The China Wall

The Timeless Legend of Johnny Bower

Johnny Bower #1

Bob Duff
with **Johnny Bower**

Foreword by
Gordie Howe® Mr. Hockey®

The China Wall

The Timeless Legend of Johnny Bower

Published by
Immortal Investments Publishing
www.immortalinvestments.com
35122 W. Michigan Avenue, Wayne, Michigan 48184
1-800-475-2066

Publisher's Cataloging-in-Publication
(Provided by Quality Books, Inc.)

Bower, Johnny, 1924-
    The China wall : the timeless legend of Johnny Bower
/ by Johnny Bower as told to Bob Duff. -- 1st ed.
    p. cm.
    LCCN 2005930099
    ISBN 0-9723637-6-9

    1. Bower, Johnny, 1924- 2. Hockey goalkeepers--
Canada--Biography. 3. Toronto Maple Leafs (Hockey
team)
    I. Duff, Bob. II. Title.

GV848.5.B685A3 2005   796.962'092
                              QBI05-600105

I dedicate this book to my family—my wife Nancy, our children John II, Cindy and Barbara, our grandchildren John III, Bruce, Kelly, Staci, Alison and Dale and to my sisters Anne, Rose, Betty and Margaret. To all of you, I say thank you for the love, respect and support you have given to me.

CONTENTS

TRUE FRIENDS—THAT'S THE BEST way I can describe the relationship between the Bowers and the Howes. Johnny Bower is one of those guys who is just like part of the family. You'd be proud to have him as a neighbor. I've never heard bad words about Johnny from anyone and that speaks very highly about his character.

I grew up in Saskatoon and Johnny's home was in Prince Albert, about 90 miles to the north. As youngsters, it was very seldom that we played against each other. He was a group ahead of me in youth hockey. He won't admit it, but he's significantly older than me. That's one thing about Johnny. There's a big question about whether he's lying about his age. I don't know what the truth is, but somebody said that he grew a beard in grade school.

The first goal I ever scored in action with the Red Wings uniform on was against Cleveland in an exhibition game. I was so proud of myself and then I found out later, the guy I scored a goal against was also from Saskatchewan. It was Johnny.

When you hear somebody is from your hometown area, it's nice to get to know them. I'd met him earlier, but there wasn't much of an association at the time, because we were basically strangers until I got married to Colleen in 1953 and she and I spent some summers in Saskatoon.

We decided that rather than stay in Saskatoon, we'd go up to Waskesiu, a resort town north of Prince Albert and maybe I would get a job on the golf course. Where we ended up settling was very close to where the Bowers lived. We stayed in a shack tent with plank wood for walls and a couple of windows. It was a rough part of the country, because if you cooked bacon, you had to lock the doors in case the bears were in the area, because they'd come right in. Johnny and his wife Nancy had a cabin, so they were the ones who were living in luxury.

We used to have a lot of fun together. We got to know one another and I've always said, "If the wives get along, then you've got yourself a good partner." Well, Nancy and Colleen got along extremely well and Johnny and I never had any troubles. We'd golf and fish, play a little bit of tennis and play catch, just like a couple of teenagers. The girls would get involved, too. We used to hit little pop flies to each other. On Saturdays, we'd go to the dances they had every week in Waskesiu.

Colleen had a friend in Nancy and I was working at the golf course. Every other day, they'd get me to change the water in the ball washers, rake the sand and then put new holes on the greens. So what I'd do is I'd tell Johnny, "I'm starting at 7:30 in the morning, you can meet me at the second hole." Then I'd play out of his bag. I'd do everything I had to do for work and we'd get a round of golf in at the same time. I was squealed upon by one of the members and the superintendent said, "Just relax. The guy who did it before you took the whole morning and two hours in the afternoon to do it. You get it all done in four hours." So they left me alone to do that and we got a lot of golf in that way.

In the shack tent, we had no place to eat. Basically, all we had was an outdoor grill, a barbecue pit was all it was, so we'd eat of lot of our meals at Bower's Big Boy, Johnny and Nancy's restaurant. And our plumbing was outside, located in an outhouse. We had to run across the road, but we were fairly close to it, thank God. When the girls were in there, we'd pretend we were bears and we'd bang up against the walls and growl and scare them. That was Johnny's idea, not mine.

We both loved to get out on the lake and fish, mostly for northern pike. On one occasion, John got so darn excited when he caught a fish, he tried to grab it with his hands. They're so slippery and this one time, he put his rod down and the son of a gun jumped right out his hand and back into the water, taking the rod with him. He had this weird look on his face and I found out he'd borrowed the rod from his neighbor. Next thing I know, he's undressing and getting ready to jump in the ice cold water to go after it. That was the most exciting moment we ever had on the boat. After we came back in from the lake, we'd usually go to Johnny's restaurant and if we'd caught any fish, Nancy would stay up late into the night to cook them for us.

When you get to know somebody and you hear other people speak of them, you really get to realize what a great guy he truly is. I don't know of anybody playing with Johnny who ever had a bad word to say about him. He's just one of those wonderful fellows who comes along that's tolerant of everything. If trouble is there, he'll enjoy it and try to find a way to get out of it. I've never seen him without a smile on his face. When his team lost, his grin was the same as when his team won. If you try 100 per cent, then you should have no bad feelings about the outcome. That was relayed to me once and I think somebody must have told Johnny the same thing. There's a good picture of us together when the Leafs won the Cup in 1963 and I've got my arm around him at center ice, congratulating him. I felt it was the right thing to do. He was an old friend and I had to go congratulate him.

There was a lot of kidding that went on between us during games. I'd go in on him and I'd score, then I'd circle the net and I'd say, "Thank you." But when he'd stop me, all he'd do was grin. One time, he stopped me in the playoffs and I let him know that I was going to throw him in Waskesiu Lake that summer. "It's out of the boat with you," I told him. One game at the old Olympia, I guess I must have hit the side or the top end of the puck, because it rotated and it died like a knuckleball. His arm came up to get it and then it dipped to about knee high and went in. That was one time when I definitely circled the net and said, "Thank you."

One time I came in and Johnny made a heck of a save,

but it was on the wrong leg. He kicked out the right leg and the puck hit the left pad. I said to him, "At least kick out the right pad. Don't make me feel bad and think you can stop it without trying." Another time I shot it and he just robbed me with his glove hand. I said, "If you look in the other hand, I bet you'll find my watch." Johnny hated giving up goals. He was so good, he could make stops in his dreams. We played Johnny and the Maple Leafs in the Stanley Cup playoffs four times and they beat us in three of those series, including the Stanley Cup finals in 1963 and 1964. Toronto had a heck of a club. They had good, solid defense, but we out shot them in quite a few of those games, so goaltending obviously had a lot to do with it.

After they beat us in the 1964 final series, I wanted Johnny's stick and I asked him for it as we shook hands. I've often done that after a series or at an All-Star Game, asked somebody whom I respected for their stick, Johnny Bucyk, Bobby Orr, Jean Beliveau, Bobby Hull and others that I think highly of. Johnny is certainly one of those players.

The last time I saw Johnny and Nancy was when I attended the 2004 All-Star game in Minnesota. Along with our Business Managers and long time friends Del Reddy and Aaron Howard, and our friend Felix Gatt, we all had a chance to reminisce in the hotel lobby. With Johnny and Nancy living in the Toronto area and Colleen and I based in Michigan, we don't see as much of each other as we did in those Saskatchewan days. Even so, the Bowers will always be our true friends.

MR. HOCKEY® GORDIE HOWE®

Mr. Hockey® Gordie Howe® is recognized as the greatest all-around player in hockey history. Playing in an astounding 32 pro seasons, he garnered 1,071 goals, appeared in a world record 29 All-Star games, and retired from the NHL at the incredible age of 52. Amazingly, he played 7 pro seasons with sons Marty and Mark, earning 2 World Championships and being named league

MVP at the age of 45.

For over 50 years, Colleen Howe Mrs. Hockey®, managed his entire career. They married in 1953, and although she suffers today from advanced dementia she is also a legend in the hockey world for her pioneering and trailblazing contributions. As the sport's first female agent and as a builder she established a legacy as the most influential woman in hockey history.

Today, their business endeavors and management are skillfully handled by their long time friends Del Reddy and Aaron Howard who continue to perpetuate the legacy of the game's greatest ambassadors—Mr. and Mrs. Hockey® Gordie and Colleen Howe.

Acknowledgements

First of all, I have to thank the legions of Toronto Maple Leafs fans for all of their support over the years.

I also must thank Jim Hendy and Norbert Stein of the American Hockey League's Cleveland Barons, who encouraged me to go to Toronto and to play my best.

I give thanks to the Toronto Maple Leafs organization and the players who I had the privilege to play with over the years.

I'd also like to thank publisher Mike Reddy, Del Reddy, Jennifer Hilliker and everyone at Immortal Investments, who made this book a reality. Also, a special thank you to Gordie Howe, Mr. Hockey for writing the Foreword and George Armstrong for contributing by writing the Tribute.

I'd like to thank my grandson John III for convincing me to tell my story and I'd also like to thank Bob Duff for helping me put my story into words.

WE ALL HAVE OUR HEROES. Maybe it was an astronaut, a movie star, or an athlete that you chose to put up on the pedestal. My hero was a goaltender—two goaltenders, actually. As an impressionable youngster growing up in the east end of the Toronto suburbs in the mid-1960s, two men caught my eye, Toronto Maple Leafs goaltenders Terry Sawchuk and Johnny Bower. To be granted the honor of relaying Johnny's story is a memory that I will always hold dear to my heart.

Each night after school, as I positioned myself in front of the makeshift net at the end of our driveway, I imagined I was one of these two legendary warriors whilst parrying the whistling drives aimed my way by my older brother.

Apparently, I was not alone in this vision quest. "Do you realize how many great saves were made in your name in driveways across the country?" a fan asked Bower once when we were out together.

Johnny and I first met in 2002 while working together on the book WITHOUT FEAR, which ranked hockey's 50 greatest goaltenders. It was a thrill to work alongside a boyhood idol and even more exciting to be given the chance to get to know someone who remains a sports icon to the masses.

The love people express for this man who hasn't put himself in the way of a puck in an NHL game since 1969 is wondrous. Watching their faces light up as they tell Bower what he's meant to their lives is nearly as amazing as the way it leaves Bower almost speechless. He is sincerely flattered to hear each tale.

When you work for a living as a sportswriter, you spend the better part of your days around spoiled, pampered millionaire athletes, many of whom don't get it. They aren't aware of the good fortune which has been bestowed upon them. Bower appreciates the warmth. "I could do this all day," he said during one book-signing appearance we made.

Bower's first pro camp in 1945 with the AHL's Cleveland Barons was held at the University of Michigan. Harvey Teno was Cleveland's goalie at the time.

"I remember going to watch the first day of camp," recalled Charlie Teno, Harvey's brother and a pretty fair goalie himself. "There was this young fellow in the other net and he was stopping everything." That fellow was Johnny Bower.

"In the car on the way home, I told Harvey he'd better look for work, because he wasn't Cleveland's goalie any more." Even though Bower took his job, he and Harvey grew to be the closest of friends. Johnny's just that kind of guy. How could you not like him?

Johnny and his wife Nancy are two of the most genuine, down-to-earth people you will ever meet. That they've welcomed me into their home and offered me the chance to tell their life story is something I will always treasure, in the same fashion that Toronto treasures Johnny.

When Bower celebrated his 80th birthday, it was front-page news in Toronto. The city held a giant party to recognize the occasion. Nearly six decades after his pro debut, the man they revered as The China Wall remains as ageless, timeless and popular as ever, the honorary grandfather of every Toronto Maple Leafs fan.

Few of us are ever granted the chance to meet our heroes. It's an even rarer occasion when the person we looked up to proves capable of living up to our lofty expectations. I've been lucky on both counts.

Sawchuk and Bower are the reasons I became a netminder—why nearly 40 years later, I still put myself in the way of rubber pucks a few times a week.

They are the root cause of the knee injuries, shoulder separations and numerous cuts, bruises and lacerations I've suffered over the years; and I've told Johnny this.

"We're just a couple of old goalies," he said.

I can't think of a more flattering compliment.

—BOB DUFF
JANUARY 2006

xvi

CHAPTER ONE

THE AGE OLD DEBATE

My name is Johnny Bower and I was born November 8, 1924 in Prince Albert, Saskatchewan.

No really, I was.

People have been trying to find out my real age for ages, it seems, but the truth of the matter is that I've been telling the truth all along. Now, getting people to believe I've been telling them the truth, well, that's an entirely different story.

Ever since I became a National Hockey League regular when the Toronto Maple Leafs drafted me from the American Hockey League's Cleveland Barons back in the spring of 1958, there's been this ongoing search to determine my actual age, as if it would be some sort of significant archeological find, like discovering who built Stonehenge or the Egyptian Pyramids. You know, some of my teammates even wondered whether I'd had a hand in the construction of those structures!

One time my age was being debated in the Leafs dressing room and I suggested that my birth certificate had been lost during the war. "Which one?" Frank Mahovlich asked. "World War I or the Boer War?" Another time with the Leafs, we were going through customs to enter the United States for a road trip when this stern-faced U.S. Customs Officer pulled me aside. "This line is only for the hockey players," he growled. "I am a player," I barked back. "No you're not. You're too old," he responded. We had quite the argument for a bit before the officer was convinced I actually was part of the team.

Over the years, a lot of the writers who were covering the Maple Leafs set out to locate my birth records and tried to get their hands on a copy of my birth certificate, but they didn't have the right documents to be able to get a copy.

Even my family encouraged the speculation. During one visit home for a family reunion, my dad said, "You know, Johnny, some nights on the television, you look like you're 56 years old." I just looked at him and said, "Some nights, I feel like it, especially when I'm getting pelted with pucks by the Chicago Black Hawks or the Montreal Canadiens." I must admit, as the years went by, I played a role in the ongoing mystery about how many years I'd been on the earth. When people would ask, I'd mess with them. I recall one time when I was closing in on my 44th birthday; Louis Cauz of the Toronto Globe & Mail was doing a story and asked me my age. "I'll be 44 next week," I told him. "And may God strike me dead if I'm lying." Then I looked skyward and added with a chuckle, "Take it easy on me Lord."

I'd tell other writers whenever they asked, "I've been lying about my age so long now, even I'm confused. Just say I'm 35 going on 40." Even the experts were uncertain. One record book would list me as being born in 1922. Another would say 1923. A third would suggest it was 1925. I liked to keep them guessing, but the truth is, it didn't matter if I told them the honest truth. They weren't going to believe it.

It all started when I was in Cleveland. They knew my right age, but all of a sudden, here comes Punch Imlach, who at that particular time was coaching Springfield. I'd enjoyed some really good success against them over the years and I guess he must have remembered that, because when Punch did get the job as assistant general manager in Toronto in 1958, the Leafs drafted me. Punch asked me, "How old are you now?" I said, "Well, I'm 34 years old." Then he said, "You've got to be kidding me. You're older than that." And I said, "No I'm not." And he says, "Well, have you got a birth certificate?" And I said, I had one, but we had a big fire in Prince Albert, the house burned down and everything went up in smoke. Nothing like that happened, to be honest with you, but I guess as the debate raged over my age, I enjoyed having a little fun with it.

Another time, Punch asked me for my birth certificate and I reminded him, "We had a big fire in the house in Prince Albert. It burnt down, we lost everything and I haven't got a birth certificate." "Well," he said. "You've got to get one and it's for your own good." I asked why and he said, "It's for your pension. (NHL president Clarence) Campbell's got to know your age." I said, "Look Punch, I think I'm 43." "Well, they don't believe that," he said. "They know you were in the army." "Yeah, but I was only there a short time," I told him. "Doesn't matter," he said. "You've got to produce a birth certificate." Well, I tried to get a fake one, but I couldn't.

The day I tried to negotiate a contract with him that season, I had some more fun with Punch. I told him I had good news for him. I'd found my birth certificate and I was actually two years younger than I thought I was. And he said, "How could you be? And where'd that birth certificate come from? You told me before that your house burned down." But I told him that was something that hadn't really happened. My dad had it all along and he gave it to me. But Punch was too smart of a guy to try to get one over on. He always had the first word and the last word. As we went on, Punch said to me, "If you have your birth certificate with you, I'll give you a $1,000 cash bonus before we even negotiate a contract." I sat there looking at him across the desk checking all of my pockets—in my shirt, in my pants—and he said, "Alright, where is it?" And I said, "Oh my gosh, I must have left it at home." He said, "I knew you we're lying Bower." I asked, "Am I still going to get the $1,000?" And he said, "No, you're not going to get that money." I only wished I'd been able to have a phony one made, because I would have fixed him good.

As for a birth certificate, I've definitely got one. In fact, when Clarence Campbell was president of the National Hockey League, we had a meeting and I asked him a question. "Mr. Campbell, any player who turns 45, can he draw a pension?" And he said, "You mean as a player?" And he looked at me and he said, "Oh Mr. Bower, it's you." Then he said, "If you can produce your birth certificate, then I'll give you a proper answer." So now it was to my own benefit to produce it so I could get my pension, so you better believe I found that birth certificate. You better believe I told the truth about my age. I got a birth certificate from Regina, the provincial capital in Saskatchewan. My wife Nancy took it and put it in the safe and it's been there ever since.

Maybe part of the problem was that I looked like I was 80 or 90 at that particular time when I was playing goal for the Leafs. I was called the Archie Moore of hockey and the Methuselah of the nets. As the years went by, Jim Proudfoot of The Toronto Star and the other newspaper guys in Toronto started making me older and older and older every year. They still do it, even today. To this day, it seems, everybody always wants to know the date of my birth, what year I was born. I've told everybody the truth the last couple of years. I turned 80 in 2004 and that's my true age. The last few charity golf tournaments I played in, during the question and answer sessions we had, people asked me, "Really, is that your true age?" And I said, "Yes it is" and everybody cheered. I guess they finally believe me.

Who knew back when I was growing up in Prince Albert that my age would become such a debate for the ages? I came from a family of one brother, Mike and seven sisters—Mary, Therisia, Anne, Helen, Rose, Betty and Margaret—the son of John and Betty Kiszkan. That's another common misconception about me that I'd like to clear up right now. My birth name was Kiszkan. My dad, John Kiszkan, he worked for Burns and Company in Prince Albert, a packing company. A lot of people think that my name became Bower because I was adopted, but that's not the case at all. There was a separation in the family later on in my youth and I eventually decided to choose my own name, which was Bower. That was the reason why my name changed. I was 21 when I legally changed my name to Bower. My sister Rose worked for a lawyer and she was the one who helped me with it.

I grew up during the Great Depression and times were tough all over. We were a poor family, like most families were at that time, but we had a lot of fun. We lived in a nice little house all pretty well gathered together. My dad was a laborer his whole life. All he ever did was work, but what I learned from him was the value of hard work. My parents taught me to keep my nose clean and treat authority figures with respect and I think that proved to be pretty solid training for a career in professional hockey.

I loved P.A. That's what everyone from out west calls Prince Albert. Prince Albert was a great place to play hockey. There was always a lot of ice for us to play on, because the temperature got to be 45-50 below zero in the winter. We played out on the roads and the city of Prince Albert would flood the back field areas in behind the schools. They'd put boards around the ice. On one side, they had skating and on the other side, we had shinny hockey and that's where we learned how to play hockey, more or less. But it was so cold that it didn't matter where you went, there was a lot of ice.

I started playing hockey when I was around 10 years old. Why I ended up being a goaltender I don't know. Whenever somebody asks me why I wanted to be a goaltender, I tell them, well, I wasn't a very good skater. I was a big kid, big boned, big structure, but for some reason, I don't know why, I didn't want to be a forward. I was stocky, but I used to watch these kids get bounced around the ice and I'd think that's crazy. I don't want any part of that. I'm going to stay in goal. It's as easy as pie. As I got older, I started to realize it wasn't so easy after all. Maybe I should have been a defenseman.

I may not know why I became a goaltender, but I'm certain as to when I became a goaltender. When we were kids, there was a chap, named Joe Halko whose dad threw a baby mattress out in the backyard for the garbage men to take away. And Joe came up with the idea to split that little mattress he had right in half, which he did and then he sewed it up. We put elastic around them, because we had no straps and we used those for goal pads and hey, it worked pretty well. I would shoot at him and then we'd switch and he would shoot at me. That's the way it all started and I felt pretty good being a goalie. I thought, hey this is great.

With no money for equipment, we learned to improvise. We played with wooden pucks a lot of the time. We didn't have real pucks or anything like that, so my dad used to cut a piece of cord wood down to the size of a puck. Then we'd get some black tape and tape it up to look like a puck. Boy, it would hurt just like a real puck when it hit you. We used to follow the horses down the road and as soon as the horses did their thing, we waited for about four or five minutes and then we had ourselves a lot of hockey pucks there, I'll tell you. We called them road apples.

Things were pretty tough and a lot of us guys didn't even have skates at the time. We just played on the river without any skates, just a pair of good heavy boots. It was great shinny hockey. My dad couldn't afford a hockey stick, but I wasn't the only kid in that situation. There were a lot of kids around the school that played after school and their dads would look around in the trees until they found a branch that was curved like a hockey stick. We had a lot of poplar trees in Prince Albert and my dad, he got one from a poplar tree. He planed it down for me and that thing, boy oh boy, maybe that's why I always played in goal, because I couldn't lift it. It was solid. I had that thing for so long. You couldn't break it, it was so thick. It was shaped really well. I played hockey with it on the road and out in the backyard on the rink.

Everybody carried a hockey stick. It was so cold on the road, especially when we were going to school, we'd find a patch of ice and just start playing hockey on the road. I met a lot of nice fellows going to school. We never had any problems with anybody. Everybody seemed to get along pretty good. There was real harmony.

I played my entire minor hockey career in Prince Albert. I worked my way up from, well they called us the peanuts when we first started out, right up through peewee and juvenile to junior. I went all the way up the ladder in Prince Albert.

Some of the teams I played for were associated with our school, St. Marks. We weren't really that big of a team, mostly farm kids, but boy did we hustle. Those farm kids, they're used to shoveling hay on the farm, so they knew how to take care of themselves. We had a few good scraps and the little guys didn't back down from anybody. They just kept on working and working and working. We had good coaching, too. A priest, Father Delisle, coached us for awhile and when he was busy with church, one of the fathers of the boys would take over behind the bench.

We did okay in our own division when we played against Flin Flon, or Battleford, or Moose Jaw, the different area teams, but Saskatoon was too powerful for us. Those fellows from Saskatoon would come in and in fact I played against Gordie Howe at that time. We just couldn't beat Gordie Howe and his teams. They had good teams, a lot of good players. We were a bunch of farm boys, more or less and they whomped us pretty good. Prince Albert was a city of only about 35,000 people and Saskatoon had 80,000. The chances of getting more players and getting better players was with Saskatoon. One time we lost 8-2 and we were lucky to get two goals against that team. Howe, he got more than a hat-trick on me, I think he ended up with five goals. I was pretty shaky, but they had such a great team, with good coaching and good passing.

Saskatoon was only 90 miles away, so we played them a lot. Gordie Howe won quite a few big games against me at that time. Even then he was big and strong, a well-built kid. At age 18 he was signed by the Detroit Red Wings. I think everyone knows what kind of a player he turned out to be. He became the greatest hockey player of all time.

When the Prince Albert Mintos senior team was practicing, I used to spend a lot of time hanging around the rink. A lot of us kids did, because that was one way to get some equipment. They'd give us their old stuff and that's how I got my first pair of skates, from a guy named Don Deacon, a left-winger who was a great hockey player. He went to Detroit to play pro in 1935 and ended up playing parts of three seasons with the Red Wings in the NHL. I used to sneak in and watch the Mintos play, especially watch the goaltenders, then later I got a job as a rink rat. That's when he gave me an old pair of his skates and they must have been size 12, because I had to stuff paper in the toes to make them fit. They were tube skates and I couldn't get used to them at all. I was supposed to have goalie skates, but at that particular time there weren't any available.

We may not have had much in the way of luxuries, but one thing we did have was a nice radio. The kids used to come down to the house on Saturday night and we'd sit down around the radio to listen to Foster Hewitt and Hockey Night In Canada. Everybody else would be cheering for the Maple Leafs and I would be cheering for Boston, whenever the Bruins were playing the Leafs. That's because I wanted to be Boston goalie Frankie Brimsek. As a kid, I worshipped him. I never saw him play, but I read a lot about him. He set a lot of records and he was a great goalkeeper for Boston. His record speaks for itself. He's in the Hockey Hall of Fame and he put up a great mark, posting a pair of three-shutout streaks during his first month in the NHL when he was called up by Boston in 1938 and he was called Mr. Zero at the time because of it. He led Boston to the Stanley Cup and won the

Calder and Vezina Trophies and was selected to the NHL First All-Star Team the same year, the first rookie goalie ever to do that. I'd think, "Someday I'm going to be like him, Mr. Zero." It didn't turn out that way, but eventually, after I ended up in Toronto, at one time, Punch wanted to trade me from Toronto to Boston for Eddie Sandford, but the deal fell through. I thought, "Wow. I'm finally going to get to play for the Bruins," but it didn't work out. I ended up staying in Toronto and I had a pretty good life with the Leafs.

The whole Mr. Zero thing, it got me mad once when I was playing in the American Hockey League with Cleveland. We were playing against Pittsburgh, which was affiliated with Toronto. They had a goaltender by the name of Gil Mayer and he wore number zero. I wore number one in Cleveland. Every time we'd play him, I'd see him wearing that zero and I'd think, "There's no way he should be wearing that number because I'm a lot better than him." This is all going through my mind, but you know, I was wrong. Gil Mayer was a pretty good goaltender in his own right.

I have to tell the truth and this probably isn't a good thing to be telling kids, but I didn't like school. I paid more attention to going out on the pond and working on my goaltending than concentrating on my education and my schoolwork. I decided that it would be better for me to make a decision as to what I was going to concentrate more on— hockey or school. I went up to Grade 11. After that, I just went out and joined up with some bigger teams that offered more experience and more competition. I started playing junior hockey when I was 17 in Prince Albert. They called us the junior Black Hawks. Louis Laroque, a local car salesman, bought the team and was the coach for a couple of seasons.

We had an army reserve unit in Prince Albert and a lot of us kids from the hockey team used to go every Friday night. We had uniforms and they trained us. It was good fun. We did that for about two or three years. It gave us kids something to do. When the war broke out, I was 15 and most of the guys joined up.

The first group went over to Vernon, B.C., but I didn't go with them because one of the generals found out how young I was. I waited for about three months and finally when another group was going, I got in with that group. I met up with most of the other guys in Vernon. It was a holding unit where they trained you. And when men were needed overseas, they called you up to go to war.

They found out when I was in Vernon, that I was too young, so I was stationed there for two years. I eventually got across to England, they were still training and I think what happened was that they had changed colonels in the holding unit. He called out my name and said, "You're ready to go, get packed and be ready in seven hours." So that was it. That's what happened. I was sent overseas when I was 18.

The unit I joined up with was called the Prince Albert Volunteers and we were put into other divisions when we got to Vernon. We were part of what they called a home unit. Another regiment stationed there was the Royal Winnipeg Rifles. They had a patch on their shoulder which read RWR and the British soldiers sure used to tease them. Run women run, they called them in England where we trained and guarded tanks.

We were stationed in Guilford, England. If somebody got sick, or got shot, or broke a leg or something like that and they needed men, they would call somebody from this home unit. They'd say, "We need six men. Give us the six best men you've got." They were taking men like that to fill out their battalions to ensure they had the right amount of men. You could hear the German planes going over all the time. It was pouring rain nearly every day and when it rains in England, boy does it rain! You know how they say it was raining frogs? I swear to God, this is a true story. We met a couple of girls coming down the road one day and we stopped to talk, which we weren't supposed to do, because the timing was supposed to be perfect, otherwise they'd figure something had gone wrong. I stopped to talk for about a minute and I asked, "What are those things hopping all over the road?" She said, "Slugs" but I couldn't understand what she was talking about. "We call them frogs in Canada," I told her.

I was put into the Second Canadian Division, as a gunner with the Queen's Own Cameron Highlanders. Our dress uniform included kilts. That was one of the divisions that went to Dieppe, France. According to the history books, when the Dieppe raid took place on August 19, 1942, 5,000 of the 6,100 troops involved were Canadian. The idea was to open a second front in Europe, but the operation was ill-fated, the worst single-day disaster for the Allied forces during World War II. The Queen's Own Cameron Highlanders and the South Saskatchewan Regiment attacked the beach at Pourville, part of a five-pronged assault. I heard how many were lost and a large part of the losses were a division from Saskatoon, the First Division Saskatoon Light Infantry.

My unit was one of the hardest hit, suffering 346 casualties according to the National Archives of Canada. Canadians suffered the brunt of the casualties at Dieppe. The National Archives note that there were 907 killed, 2,460 wounded and 1,874 taken prisoner. Quite a few of the boys from Prince Albert that went to Dieppe (including some of the guys I'd played hockey with), didn't come back. There were some good players from our team who got killed there; many were killed before they even hit the beach.

If I had been healthy I would have gone, but I wasn't even close. Even though I went over to England, it ended up that I didn't see action at all, I got sick there in the damp weather. We were taking training in Vernon, B.C. and when we got over there, we had to do some different training all together. We had to do group marches, going through water with your rifle up in the air, because in war time, that was something that could happen to you, no matter where they sent you. That's where I got sick. So I was held back from Dieppe.

We started going on maneuvers again for more training and that's when I really got sick. I had a lot of problems in my back and my hands. They'd swell up. They gave me lots of treatments, heat treatments under the lamps, therapy. No pills though, which was great. I've never liked taking pills. The nurses used to massage my hands. I was doing all kinds of exercises to massage my hands, but it was getting to the point where I couldn't do it and I just lost interest in everything. They said it was rheumatoid arthritis right off the bat. The arthritis was hitting me all over my body for awhile there. When you get arthritis in your hands, especially your knuckles, wow, your hands get pretty sore. I'd get swollen knuckles all the time and sometimes, my hands would go completely numb. But eventually when I got older, especially once I started playing goal for a living, I got used to pain. It's like nothing. You know it's there. It's just throbbing, throbbing, throbbing. I had my hands bandaged up really good when I was playing. Bobby Haggert, our trainer in Toronto, used to do a fabulous job of bandaging up my fingers, especially my middle fingers. Nobody knew it, that I couldn't shoot a puck too well because of arthritis.

They sent me to hospital in Birmingham, England. I was there for about three weeks and then they sent me to another hospital. I kept going from one hospital to another and I guess it got to the point where they just gave up on me. "It's time for you to be an orderly," they decided, but I didn't want to be an orderly. I didn't want to clean all those pots and pans.

The army even promoted me, but I didn't care for that, either. They made me a Lance Corporal, but I didn't like trying to order the other fellows to wash dishes and that kind of stuff, so in a couple of weeks, I turned in my stripe and said I didn't want it.

When I look back on it today, arthritis may have saved my life. That's what I've told my wife Nancy several times. But I wasn't even thinking about that. You're going there to fight for your country like everyone else and if you go into action, well that's it. You just hope and pray that nothing happens to you.

Eventually, they sent me back to Regina to work as an orderly in 1944. I could have stayed there for another six months, but I said, "No, I don't want to be an orderly." So I got my discharge and came back to Saskatoon.

Then I went back to Prince Albert and got a job on the railroad. There was a lot of jobs available at that time, because they were still fighting over in Europe and the Pacific. I took a course as a boilermaker.

All of a sudden, since I was only 19, it was pointed out to me that I had another year of junior hockey left. Nobody knew how, but I did. It was because I'd lied about my age to get into the army. You can certainly understand why there was such confusion. No one could figure out how I could be in the army for four years and still be eligible for junior hockey, since you had to be 18 to join the armed forces and you needed to be under 20 to play junior. It was quite the controversy for awhile, but I produced my birth certificate and I was cleared to play. I knew that piece of paper would come in handy someday and it sure did for me that winter, because it was during that season when the scout from the Cleveland Barons saw me playing.

CHAPTER TWO

AT HOME IN CLEVELAND

After I produced my birth certificate, the Saskatchewan Amateur Hockey Association determined everything was legitimate and I spent the 1944-45 season playing for the Prince Albert Black Hawks of the Saskatchewan Junior Hockey League. I even led the league with a 2.57 goals-against average.

It was late in the season when I met a scout by the name of Hub Wilson and he asked me if I'd be interested in going up to the Cleveland Barons of the American Hockey League. I said, "I don't know." I had a good job with Canadian National Railway and I didn't want to leave it. First of all, I wanted to see if I could get permission from the railroad. I told him, "If I could get a leave, I will go." So I got a six-month leave from CNR and I went down to their training camp.

Around the same time, Eddie Shore approached me about signing with Springfield, another AHL franchise, but I'd heard stories that he was a real tough guy. Once in a while, he'd chain his goalies up to the net, tie them to the crossbar so they couldn't fall down when he felt they were falling down too much. I got scared, because I was a flopper, so I figured, "No, I'll go to Cleveland instead."

I wasn't sure whether I was going to make the grade or not. That's why I took the leave from the railroad. Coming right out of junior hockey, stepping up to the American League, being right next to the National Hockey League, that's a pretty big step to make, especially when you don't have the right equipment.

The last year of junior hockey when I played goal for the Prince Albert Black Hawks and then in Cleveland, I went there with my tube skates, the same ones that Don Deacon had given me, the only skates I'd ever been able to call my own. I went to the first practice and the trainer said to me, "What are those?" and I said, "They're my skates." He said, "You can't use those here." I said, "Why not?" and he said, "Because they aren't proper skates for use here. Remember, you're in the American Hockey League now. You can't use tube skates to play goal at this level of hockey."

They took my antiques and threw them away. They gave me a brand new pair of goalie skates. Well, I didn't like those goalie skates at all. I couldn't get used to them. They were lower to the ice and had a lot heavier boot than I was used to wearing. But I soon discovered they made my lateral movement much quicker and once I got to know how my feet fit in the boots and how to work with them, it made a big difference in my game.

The funny thing is, as my career continued, I was very, very fussy with my equipment. I liked doing things myself. I didn't want anybody touching my equipment, or my gloves, or my stick, or anything like that. I was very meticulous when I put on my gear before the game. I'd wear my right pad loosely and my left pad snug. I felt I could kick out my left leg quicker if the pad was tight to the leg, but the right one had to be loose or I didn't feel right. I developed a habit of pounding my right pad three or four times with my stick at every stoppage, to knock it back into position because I wore it so loose. I'd never wear tape inside my skate, even if I had a foot or ankle injury. It just felt too uncomfortable. Maybe it's just habits you develop, but another thing I knew was when it came time to playing the game, If anybody touched my sticks I would know it and I would get a little perturbed. I would have to get over it pretty quickly though, because we had a game to play.

I was particular about my sticks, too. The trainers used to come in and tape my sticks and I just didn't like the way they did it. I told them, "Look, leave my sticks alone if you don't mind, I'd like to do it." I liked the feel of my stick. I didn't like the 38-40 ounce stick. I liked a 28-30 ounce stick at the most, because my wrists and hands were weaker than most goalies due to arthritis. And Mr. Jim Hendy, who was one of my general managers in Cleveland told me, "I'll get you any kind of sticks you want, as long as you stop those pucks." And he did.

I went for a tryout at Cleveland's training camp in October of 1945 in Ann Arbor, Mich. and I made the team. I made the grade at training camp. When I got to Cleveland, there was a guy by the name of Harvey Teno in goal. He was a small, pudgy guy, but he was good. He'd been the regular goaltender for Cleveland during the 1944-45 season, when the Barons won the Calder Cup title. I alternated with him that first season, then I replaced him. In camp that first season, besides Harvey Teno they had another guy, Al Tomori, a young goaltender and a pretty good one. He was a lot younger than me. They were going to develop him instead of me. But he was lacking in experience, so they stuck with me.

Seventeen hundred dollars was my salary for that first year. And with my first contract, I got fifty dollars as my signing bonus. That's right, fifty bucks. Kind of pales in comparison to what the big stars get for signing a deal today, doesn't it? But I tell you what, walking home with fifty dollars in my pocket, it felt pretty good. But when I showed the wad of bills to my dad, he was perplexed. "Where'd you get that money?" he demanded to know. "From Cleveland," I said. "It's a bonus for signing my contract." "They don't give you money for signing your name," he said. "You take that money back." Well, I didn't take it back. I kept ten dollars for myself and gave the other forty to my sister.

Right before I got to Cleveland, they had a goaltender by the name of Moe Roberts and he gave me a puck that was the first shutout puck that he got when he played for the team. I didn't know his background that well, but I did know he was a top-notch goaltender for Cleveland for many years. He was the No. 1 goalie for the Barons from 1933-42. And as it turned out, he wasn't done playing.

Roberts was working as an assistant trainer with the Chicago Black Hawks and on November 25, 1951, when Chicago goalie Harry Lumley was injured, Roberts donned the pads and played a shutout third period in Chicago's 5-2 victory over the Detroit Red Wings. He even stopped Gordie Howe on a breakaway, which was pretty good, considering he was 45 years old and hadn't played a game since 1946.

His actual age that night was 45 years, 11 months and 12 days, which made him the oldest goalie in the history of the NHL—even older than me, if you can believe it. I played my final NHL game in 1969 at the age of 45 years, one month and two days.

I made my debut for Cleveland in a 4-3 loss to the Hershey Bears October 16, 1945. Nick Damore, whose AHL records for wins and shutouts I would eventually shatter, was the opposing netminder. We played to a 1-1 tie at Hershey the next night, then the Barons switched to Harvey Teno between the pipes. I waited until December 1 to record the first of what would become a professional hockey record 706 victories, a 4-3 verdict over the Providence Reds. A week later, I blanked the Buffalo Bisons 2-0 for the first of what was 45 career AHL shutouts.

Those first few years in Cleveland were a tough go. I was pretty inexperienced and back then, a goalie didn't get much coaching. You were pretty much on your own to succeed or else. I had to pick up things by watching other goalies, particularly Pittsburgh's Baz Bastien.

We had different goaltenders come in, looking to take my job. Cleveland made a deal with Pittsburgh for Roger Bessette and we alternated for three seasons. Al Rollins came in and left to go to Toronto. That was during the 1949-50 season. I didn't realize it at the time, but I found out years later that the Maple Leafs were looking for a goalie to succeed Turk Broda and they were trying to decide between Rollins and myself. Squib Walker, a Toronto scout, watched six Cleveland games that season. Rollins and I alternated and they chose Rollins. Nine years later, Toronto finally got it right and picked me up. I'm just kidding, Al Rollins was a great goalie. He won a Vezina Trophy and Stanley Cup with Toronto and captured the Hart Trophy as NHL MVP with Chicago, just the second goalie in league history to do so.

Other goaltenders came in before they made the decision to go with me. I was struggling, but I never gave up and eventually I made it. I had difficulty with my rebound control when I first turned pro, but I learned to catch the puck more and that made a big difference, because Cleveland was looking to replace me with another goalie if I didn't improve my work there.

Another area where I needed to improve was in my attitude. I was a bad loser and sometimes, I was too harsh with my teammates when they made a mistake that cost me a goal. One time I complained to Geoffrey Fisher, the reporter who covered the Barons for the Cleveland News and boy, did some of the guys ever get angry with me. I learned a valuable lesson about the importance of being a team man.

It was tough slugging there for me for awhile. At first, being single at the time, the guys took me under their wing pretty good. They tried to initiate you by going out together after the game and going out to the hotel and have a few beers, but I didn't drink. I didn't even like beer. In fact, I hated beer. I was a loner more than anything. After the games on the road, I used to help the trainer hang up the equipment. In Toronto, they had their own staff of kids there to help them hang up and dry out the stuff, but in Cleveland, he was pretty much on his own.

Eventually, I got to know the other players pretty well. Once you start rooming with a certain guy, you start forgetting about those feelings. You're still lonely at times, you still miss home, it's like going away on a trip and not seeing your dad or your sisters for a long time. But when you come back home, they love to see you. After a year, it wasn't too bad. I knew what to expect, I knew what training camp was like and I knew what they expected of me. I didn't care about anybody else. I just worried about myself, trying to keep in shape. We were allowed ten pounds overweight during the summer, but I'd never go more than six. I wasn't ever heavy.

Al Sutphin was the owner of the hockey team and we all called him "Red Tie" because he always wore a suit and the tie was always red. At Christmas time, everybody would get a red tie from him, plus a bonus of maybe $50 or something. We'd have a banquet and the money would always be in an envelope under the dinner plates. To me, he was a great person to play for. He never bothered anyone. He used to smoke these big cigars a lot. He'd come in the dressing room and he'd just say, "Good luck guys, win or lose." He owned the Sutphin and Gray Ink Plant behind the arena as well. You couldn't ask for a nicer manager. He had a place in Florida and he had a motel there too and anytime you wanted to go, you were welcome. My wife Nancy and I went once and spent a week at his place there. We toured around the state a little bit. For all the years I was there, Mr. Sutphin was great to us. Everybody liked him. I still get a Christmas card from his son.

He'd brought Bun Cook in as coach in 1943 and he was a great coach. He was just like a father to you. He treated you just like you were his son. He treated everybody that well. He was a great guy. I can't say enough about him. He was the one who actually taught me how to play the angles. I used to play very deep in my net and was a reflex goaltender. He said, "If you want to play in the National Hockey League, you've got to learn to stand up and cut off the angles. You've got to come out really slowly and challenge the shooter." So after practice, he'd have me out there for five or 10 minutes and he'd be shooting pucks at me from bad angles and he said, "That's what I want you to do. From now on, we're going to work on it in practice. Don't change your game, because I like it, I just want you to improve on your angles." I didn't know anything about that. Nobody ever told me anything about playing goal growing up. I just stayed in my little square where I thought I belonged. He said, "Don't worry, I'll work with you." I got in my net and he told me to get in my crease. I did and then he told me to start coming out toward him. I did and he said, "I can't see anything now. The only thing that I can see is a little bit of the short side, so you've got to move over an inch or two." The strong side, you've got your pad, your glove and your stick available, so it's very difficult to beat a goaltender to that side. The other side, your stick side, it's very difficult to get over there quickly, so you've really got to hold the post fairly tight on that side. I used to go out too quickly and he'd say, "Whoa, you're moving too fast. Just glide out. Push yourself and close your legs and keep coming like that." He'd say, "Stop" and I would stop and then I would go back. I'd have to make sure I was covering the post on the short side. Sometimes he'd tell me to stop and he'd say, "See how far away from the post you are? You're swaying your back too much. Just make one push with your skate and keep your legs together, then coast back in and your reflexes will be a lot better for you to kick out at the puck." I listened to him and he helped me a great deal as I learned how to play my angles. Any goaltender will tell you that sometimes, you lose your angle. Many times in Toronto, I had to get out there and work on improving my angles. Some of the players would stay on the ice and help me.

Bun Cook knew where the weaknesses were with goaltenders, because he was such a great scorer with the New York Rangers in the 1920s and thirties. He played on that sensational forward line in New York with his brother

Bill and Frank Boucher. He had a terrific slap shot. He hit the goal post once while shooting at me and the puck split in two. And he could put the puck through a knot hole when he shot it. We all knew you could learn a lot from somebody like that. He had all the experience in the world. To get trained by somebody like that, I thought, "This is going to be great." We won four Calder Cups with Bun Cook as coach. He knew every mistake. He was very smart. We'd have our meetings and he'd tell the shooters where to go on the other team's goalie. The guys would listen to him, because they knew he knew what he was talking about.

I came to really like Cleveland. The city had good people and it was a good hockey town. They were drawing 12,000-13,000 people there all the time and Mr. Sutphin had good people working for him. What I liked about Cleveland particularly were the fans. They were great. They weren't what you'd call die-hard fans, because every year, you'd see a lot of new faces, but they'd give you a lot of credit if you worked hard. They'd give you a good round of applause and if you let in a bad goal, they didn't boo you as much as they did in other places. I loved Cleveland. It was a great spot to play hockey and to have the opportunity to get a job. The organization would help look for homes for the players and their wives. They really went first class for everything. A lot of guys who came in were married and if they didn't know whether they were going to stay, they stayed in a hotel room for a week or two and Mr. Sutphin took care of the bill until they found a place for them.

They had a public address announcer they'd brought in from Calgary, Gale Egan and he'd explain the rules of the game to the fans, things like offside, while the game was going on. Eventually, the team decided the fans were educated enough on the game and they stopped the announcements.

One of my teammates the first two seasons in Cleveland was Les Cunningham. He'd played in the NHL with the New York Americans and Chicago and was nearing the end of his career, but he was a great, great hockey player. Not a great skater, but he had a powerful shot. He was all wrists and very difficult to stop. He was a five-time all-star and the first player in American Hockey League history to collect 200 career points, so they named the most valuable player trophy after him in 1947. Starting in 1955-56, I won the Les Cunningham Trophy as AHL MVP three seasons in a row, the only player in AHL history ever to do that. Not too many guys can say they've won an award named after one of their teammates.

Cleveland wasn't affiliated with any NHL team, so Mr. Sutphin was free to acquire anyone he wanted and he wasn't afraid to go out and acquire veteran players. In the six-team league, the NHL farm systems were so deep they could send anybody down. They could trade three or four guys for one guy if they wanted to, because they had so many good players in the minors. I guess management felt that (players aged 29, 30), "We'll send them down and we'll get some young kids to develop." That's the way the system worked in those days. Whoever was available that was over 30 years of age, Mr. Sutphin was right there to grab them.

I had Babe Pratt and Joe Cooper, two longtime National Hockey Leaguers, as defensemen one season. They were getting over the hill, so we made a deal for them. We'd do that a lot, give an NHL team a couple of young players that they wanted in exchange for some veterans. Pratt's in the Hall Of Fame now and was an NHL All-Star and the Hart Trophy winner with Toronto in 1943-44. He paired with Cooper and boy were those guys big. Pratt used to catch a lot of pucks for me, he had the experience. Cooper was sort of a choppy skater, but a good safe player.

Pratt was quite a character and had a reputation as a carouser, but actually with us, he was sort of a loner. He and Cooper, they sort of stuck together, but in the dressing room, Pratt was a jolly sort of guy. He loved to crack jokes and he had a bundle of them. We'd go out on the road once in a while and he would join us, but not too often. After he retired, he went to Vancouver and did some scouting for the Canucks. When I used to scout for Toronto, I'd bump into him and we'd sit together, but you couldn't watch the game, because he was always telling jokes.

We were always acquiring players of that caliber to make the team better. Another legend we added was Bryan Hextall, who won the NHL scoring title with the New York Rangers in 1941-42. He was only with us for a couple of seasons, but boy he was tough. He was dynamite, absolutely tough as nails. We were sure glad to have him on our team, because there were a lot of other teams with tough players, but they sure gave him a lot of room. You didn't fool around with the Hextalls, because they were tough. It carried on for two more generations with Bryan's sons Bryan Jr. and Dennis and then Ron, who was the son of Bryan Hextall Jr. They were all good hockey players and they all played in the NHL.

They also could have called the Barons the cradle of coaches, because many of the guys I played with later coached in the NHL, some of them against me when I was with the Leafs. That would include Fred Glover, who coached Oakland and Los Angeles and Jackie Gordon, who was in charge of Minnesota, as was Glen Sonmor. Then there was Fred Shero, who guided the Philadelphia Flyers to back-to-back Stanley Cups in 1973-74 and 1974-75.

One of the reasons I think we enjoyed so much success in Cleveland was because there was genuine harmony within the team. From the trainer right up, we all seemed to mold like a family, ready to help each other out. We never flew too much, we'd always take buses and trains. We'd play cards together. One guy would buy a paper and we'd switch that paper around amongst all the players. The next time, another guy would buy the paper. Little things like that helped us bond as a team.

When it came to roommates, Bun felt that it was best to mix up the players. He'd say, "You're going to be with Freddie Glover for a couple of games. Then you're going to go with Bo Elik." I roomed pretty well with all the guys. I think it was better that way, because you'd get to know all the guys. Sometimes, teams get too cliquey when they go the other way, where you room with the same guy all season. When you break things up, I think you're better off and your team will play better hockey.

We rolled off a 30-game unbeaten streak in 1947-48 and my goals-against average of 2.68 was second-best in the league. I was part of my first Calder Cup championship team that spring, but I watched while Roger Bessette played all the games. It was understandable. He'd been selected to the AHL Second All-Star Team that season and was the more experienced goalie. I was still learning on the job.

As soon as the season ended, Bob Solinger (who I played junior with in Prince Albert and joined Cleveland the same year I did) and I jumped in our car and made the 2,800-mile trek to Prince Albert in three days. We had to dig our car out of the snow nine times along the way, but we didn't have a choice. Bobby was getting married in May and we had to get him home. Little did I know I'd be walking down the aisle before long, too.

In the summer, I was an assistant pro at the golf course in Waskesiu National Park, about 50 miles north of Prince Albert. I was there with Johnny Chad, who played for Providence and was the head pro. One day, there were these six girls who came up to the golf course and they drove me crazy. They wanted to go golfing in the afternoon. They paid their fees and all of a sudden Johnny, the pro, spotted them and told me, "Look, you better go tell those girls to watch it. The way they're swinging those clubs around, they're going to kill each other or somebody's going to get hurt." So I went out to the first tee to tell them. I told them not to swing the clubs so close to each other and to make sure they didn't stand in front of the person who was hitting the ball, but to make sure they were somewhere where they could be seen. They didn't like it and I remember I got a dirty look from this one girl named Nancy. It took them a long time to get off that first tee. Luckily, it was in the afternoon and there was nobody there. They had all of the course to themselves pretty well, which was good, because I think it took them eight hours to play eight holes.

That night, I was in town and I bumped into the girls and I said, "Hi, How are you? Are you going to the show?" They said they were and I said I was going to the show alone, so I asked Nancy if she'd like to go with me. She looked at the other five girls and I said, "I'm not paying for them too." It was 25 cents to get in. That was a lot of money in those days. Anyway, Nancy said, "Yes" and we went to the show and that was how we first got to know each other.

We started corresponding after that. She lived in Saskatoon and I lived in Prince Albert, so I used to take the train down to see her. I met her dad and mom. Her dad was a strict man, an armed forces man, Sergeant Major Frank Brain. Her mom, Esther, was a wonderful person. I always got along with Nancy's mom. After a few months we got to know each other, I said, "Nancy, I've got to go now. Everything's closed up at the lake and I've got to head back to Cleveland to play hockey, but I'd like you to marry me." She said, "You'll have to come and talk to my parents first." So I took a train to Saskatoon and met with her mom and dad and we talked about it. Her dad said, "You're a hockey player. Well, how much money do you make?" I said, "I don't know" and he said "And you want to marry my daughter?" "Yes sir," I said. "I think in time, hockey could really pay off." He said, "I'm not worried about in time. I want to know what's going to happen to her right now." I said, "We'll be fine sir. I want to marry your daughter." He sat there for the longest time, looking sternly at me and then he finally said, "What do you think, mother?" Well, Nancy's mom, she got up and I didn't know whether she was going for a gun or what she was going to do. She opened these big French doors into the next room. She went in and got this piece of paper and she gave it to Nancy. "You'll need this," she said. "It's your birth certificate." That was her seal of approval. Oh, what a relief that was to me.

I'd only known Nancy for six months when we got married in Cleveland. I told Bun Cook that I was going to get married and that I think I'd like to get married in Cleveland. He looked at the schedule and said, "Well, we've got a week off in early November, so I think I can give you a few days off if you want." That was unheard of in those days, a player getting time off to be married, but that shows you how things were different in Cleveland. I said, "Fine" and told Nancy. She came down on the train about four days ahead of the wedding date and her parents arrived in time for the ceremony.

We made it official November 3, 1948 at noon at Cleveland's Trinity Church. My teammate Roy Kelly stood up for me as best man and all my teammates attended the ceremony. Bun Cook scheduled our practice for 10 a.m. that day so everyone could make the wedding. Our captain, Fred Thurier, provided our limousine service. Freddy the Fox, we called him and he drove a big convertible. On our wedding day, he said, "There's nobody who will be allowed to drive in that convertible except Nancy and Johnny." He drove us around Cleveland from the church right to the Belmont Hotel for the reception.

Before the wedding, I took Nancy's father out, because I figured I'd better get on the good side of this old boy. I took him to a place across the road from the arena to have a beer. He liked that really strong, warm English beer. He ordered Black Forest Ale and had about three or four of them. Well, when he got up the next morning, he was really feeling it.

The only letdown on the day was that Nancy was really disappointed in the cake. In Canada, the tradition is to have fruitcake for a wedding cake. Well, they'd baked us a big, white cake for the wedding and I didn't know it wasn't a fruitcake, so when I went to cut it, I went right through it with the knife and just about wrecked the whole cake.

Bun Cook told us, "If you guys want to go to New York for a couple of days, you go ahead." But Nancy didn't want to go because she liked Cleveland. She said, "There's a lot of good stores in Cleveland. Why should I go to New York?" I thought I was going to get a little holiday away from the players, but I didn't, so naturally I had to go back after a couple of days.

During that 1948-49 season it would prove to be a breakthrough year for me as a pro. I was sharing time with Roger Bessette again, but he suffered a leg injury early in the season. That gave me a real opportunity. I started 20 straight games and made the job my own. I won my first four starts and posted back-to-back shutouts, 4-0 over New Haven and 3-0 over St. Louis, the first time a Cleveland goalie had accomplished that feat since Moe Roberts in 1936. I also lost the first teeth of my pro career, sacrificing two front teeth when clipped by a stick in a 10-6 win over Providence. I didn't get my two front teeth back for Christmas, but I did get another shutout. On Christmas Day, I blanked Indianapolis 4-0. The Capitals' goalie, Terry Sawchuk, who would later be my teammate in Toronto, skated the length of the ice to shake my hand. I don't know what it was, but I seemed to have a lot of luck on holidays. I posted a shutout on New Year's Eve in 1945 and hung up another zero on Christmas Day 1946.

When the playoffs rolled around, there were more changes. For the first time, Bun Cook went with me as his post-season goalie. I lost my debut against Springfield 8-4, making 40 saves in the loss, but then we rallied to win the series in three games. We lost to Hershey in the second round, but I'd finally established myself as Cleveland's No. 1 goalie. The Cleveland News described me as, "A spry young man with lightning reflexes." Imagine that. Someone referring to me as a young man.

I was becoming quite the business mogul in the summer months. At first, Nancy and I went into business with another couple, Ken and Jean Turnbull, opening up a restaurant in Waskesiu called the Saratoga. The men did the cooking and the women waited tables. We told them not to wear their wedding rings at work, because they'd get better tips and it worked. The tips were pretty good.

Later on, I opened up my own coffee shop at Waskesiu Lake, a hamburger joint. I used to have the best hamburgers in town. I'd buy a pound of hamburger and add two pounds of bread crumbs to it and about two eggs. But the kids sure loved them. Bower's Big Boys they were called. It was twenty-five cents for a hamburger, seventy-five cents for bacon and eggs and ten cents for a coffee. I used to be in the kitchen, doing the cooking, but I had to hire a lady to bake the pies. I enjoyed it.

Every summer I'd come down and open up the coffee shop. Later on, I went into the hotel business with Bob Webb. I was into that for a couple of years, but I didn't like it and ended up selling my share to Bob. You cater more to people who want to have a nice meal, a beer or a glass of wine. You had to go to work all dressed up and I didn't like that. The coffee shop, I could go to work in blue jeans and most of my clientele were teenagers and they were fun. I had a juke box in the corner and boy that thing would drive me crazy. I think it was only a nickel a record at the time, yet it paid half of my rent in the building, so I'd keep that machine going all day long. I enjoyed owning the restaurant. I looked forward to going up there every summer. I'd meet a lot of kids and I used to get a lot of hockey players coming up from Saskatoon and Regina, because they had a great golf course in Waskesiu, one of the best. We decorated it with autographed pictures from the hockey players I knew and that served as another attraction to bring in the people. As soon as Labor Day came along, we closed up the restaurant and got ready to go back to Cleveland.

When we returned to Cleveland in the fall of 1949, there'd been a change at the top. Mr. Sutphin sold the team to Jim Hendy, who came in from New York and took over. Jim Hendy was a great guy, too. He was really good to the guys and good to the wives, too. He knew the wives had a big responsibility, probably just as much as the players did. You know the wives, they had to watch over us and take care of us and cook for us and get us out of bed and make sure the kids stayed out of trouble and everything else. I think he had an agreement with the wives. He must have got them together behind our backs, because I'll tell you, they sure took care of us. There was no fooling around. It was all strictly hockey. And I'll tell you, Nancy was certainly a big boost to my career and my self-confidence.

We enjoyed our life in Cleveland. The people that we met were wonderful people. They were so friendly to us and they were friendly to Nancy. The hospitality was just super. We met people there that we became very good friends with for many years. There was one couple there, we got to know these people really well. Their names were Cecile and Fred Fuldauer. They were really ardent hockey fans. He was general manager of a chain of grocery stores. His wife, she just thought the world of Johnny Bower. This particular game, I was having a rough time of it, gave up a couple of quick goals in the first period and this one guy in the crowd, he yells, "Bower, you bum" and this and that and she couldn't stand it any longer. At that time, the women really dressed up to go to the games and she wore the shoes with the really high heels. She took her shoe off and cuffed this guy right in the side of the head with it. There was blood coming down his face and he stood up and it looked like there was going to be a fight in the crowd for a while until he realized it was a woman who hit him and he figured he'd better sit down. She was lucky she wasn't charged, today, she would have been for sure. But there was no way she was going to let him get away with what he said about me. He kept quiet for the final two periods.

We played an exhibition game against the Detroit Red Wings. I blocked 59 shots and we managed a 4-4 tie. My old nemesis Gordie Howe, of course, he scored a goal on me. It seemed like he always did whenever we played against each other. That was the year when we traded Al Rollins, my understudy, to Toronto. The Leafs were looking for a goalie because Turk Broda had been suspended by Leafs owner Connie Smythe, who felt Broda was too fat. Bun Cook had decided he was abandoning his two-goalie system. We finished first during the regular season, I led the AHL with 38 wins and five shutouts and we marched all the way to the Calder Cup finals before we were out-dueled by Terry Sawchuk and the Indianapolis Capitals.

The Barons were still unhappy with my rebound control. My old idea was that the defensemen cleared the puck, but I had to learn to catch more shots. It was difficult because of my arthritis, but I had to learn if I wanted to keep my job. They brought in Lou Crowdis to challenge me for my spot at training camp in the fall of 1950. I was told that Mr. Hendy favored Crowdis, but Bun Cook was in my corner. What settled it was an exhibition game against the Chicago Black Hawks. Crowdis started and surrendered four goals in the first half of the game. I shut Chicago out during my 30 minutes and the job remained mine. Crowdis was farmed out to Denver of the United States League. What I didn't tell them was I played that game with a serious leg injury and kept playing with it through the first few weeks of the season. Pro hockey was a cut-throat business in those days and you didn't dare give anyone an opening to take your place.

I caught fire that season and really found my game. I was maturing as a goaltender and my confidence just soared, especially when Bun Cook started comparing me to my hero, Frankie Brimsek, who'd been Bun's teammate in Boston. "It's amazing to me how much alike they are," he told the Cleveland News. "Both have big hands. Both work hard and fast. In fact, I think Bower is the fastest man in front of the nets since Brimsek. They both have that same type of temperament and both have that same dogged determination that goes with a will to win."

Playing goal for Cleveland was never an easy task, because the Barons believed in an attacking, up-tempo brand of hockey and that meant the goalie was often left hanging out to dry. We were almost always outshot, but at least my efforts were being appreciated. "Whoever plays goal for us doesn't get the protection some other fellows get," Bun Cook told the Cleveland News. "Johnny is frequently left back there on his own and he does a fine job. Johnny has saved our lives many times." Even opponents were taking notice. "We throw everything at Bower but the goal judge and he's always in the way," Pittsburgh's Baz Bastien said.

My 44 wins led the league and I was named to the AHL's Second All-Star Team. We were back in the Calder Cup finals, this time against the Pittsburgh Hornets and it was a tremendously competitive series. I made 50 saves in the opener, but we lost 3-2. We rebounded for a 5-4 win in Game 2, but the next game, even though I stopped 52 shots, we were hammered 9-2. Then we gained the upper hand, with 4-1 and 3-1 wins, but the Hornets outshot us 45-15 in Game 6 and stayed alive with a 3-1 triumph. It all came down to Game 7 and despite being outshot 39-17, we came away 3-1 winners and were Calder Cup champions. Winning a championship at any level, is a wonderful feeling. Starting with that season, we had a good run there for about four or five years, just like we had in Toronto in the 1960s when we won those four Stanley Cups. We had the youth, we had the experience and we had the goaltending. Mr. Hendy would always keep us fresh, get us one or two new faces every year, just to change things around. And the players, believe me, they didn't mind coming at all because you were treated so well in Cleveland. Mr. Hendy didn't want to send anybody out or trade anybody, but when he did, he would trade them to a good team, to a lower team where they'd get some ice time.

We were back on our game again in the years 1951-52 and so was I. About the only thing I lost that season was another tooth, sacrificed when I was kicked in the mouth by a skate during a 5-1 win over Indianapolis. For the first time in my career, I captured the Harry (Hap) Holmes Memorial Award as the AHL's leading goaltender. It was big news in Cleveland, because I was the first Barons goalie to win the trophy and Holmes was a Hall Of Fame former NHL goalkeeper who had first brought pro hockey to the city in 1929. I was selected to the AHL First All-Star Team and in separate polls of the coaches and players conducted by the Cleveland Plain Dealer, I was also voted to their version of the All-Star Team. The newspaper also conducted a fan vote to determine the Barons' MVP and I received 1,919 of 2,552 ballots cast. "He is the best in the league," Bun Cook said of me to the Cleveland News. "I certainly think he's the top goaltender in all of hockey right now."

We lost to Providence in the first round of the playoffs and their general manager Terry Reardon wasn't very kind in his assessment of our club. "They're slow. They move down the ice like maple syrup in the Antarctic," he told the Cleveland News. "They're lucky to have a goaltender like Johnny Bower and a coach like Bun Cook."

I had another reason to dislike Providence and it was behind me. Specifically, the goal judge who worked two periods at my end of the rink when we played there. Every time they'd score a goal, he'd shoot chewing tobacco at you. When they were just about to take a shot at you, there was an opening in the chicken wire and he'd let me have it. He didn't actually hit me in the neck, but he hit me all over the back of my sweater. I went after him a couple of times, but he was a lot older than I was, so I didn't want to swing my stick at him. But we had some good exchanges of words over the years. I asked him once why he did that and he said he just didn't like goaltenders. "I'm a Rhode Island Reds fan," he told me.

Another guy in Providence who got on my nerves was a fan who'd throw his hat on the ice whenever the Reds would score. He'd spin it out there so it would land right in front of me. I'd be mad about the goal being scored and I'd go to whack the hat with my stick and it would move. The guy had a piece of fishing line rigged to the hat. Eventually, we figured that out and the guys would grab the hat, so the team would offer ten bucks to any player who returned the hat to the penalty box. Well, after that, there were some pretty good battles over that hat. Some nights, we'd come out of there with forty or fifty bucks to spend after the game.

There was disappointment in the city when our reign as champs concluded, but the Barons organization was dreaming of bigger and better things. They applied to go into the National Hockey League, but they were refused because of the size of the arena. It only held 13,000 and you had to have at least 15,000-16,000 seats to get into the National

Hockey League. Renovations would have cost a lot of money. The shareholders said, "Why go in the National Hockey League? We're drawing 13,000 people, we're doing very well." So that fell out on us that year. Besides, the NHL didn't seem all that interested in having us aboard. "They had too little working capital," was NHL president Clarence Campbell's assessment of our bid to become part of the NHL family.

I felt that it was a mistake to write the city off as quickly as the NHL did. Cleveland operated as if it were an NHL franchise. It was a first-class team. When I was there, there wasn't anybody who complained. When they said there was a spot vacant for you in Cleveland, they'd just say, "Hey, how do we get there? Can we go to the training camp?" A lot of time when I came home, I talked about the team and how it was so successful down there, how could you go wrong? I'd talk to players about things like that and I'd tell them, "If you ever get a scout from Cleveland interested in you, tell him you'll go."

Our setback in the 1951-52 playoffs turned out to be a blip on the radar screen. We were right back on top in 1952-53. I was the AHL's First All-Star Team goalie for the second year in a row and that was also the season that I picked up my nickname.

There was a guy by the name of Geoffrey Fisher, who covered the team for the Cleveland News and I'll never forget him. He even once put on the gear and gave goaltending a try during one of our practices. I had put a shutout sequence together during the season and one morning, I picked up the paper and he'd called me China Wall Bower. Up until then, I was known as the Panther Man, but I loved my new handle. It made me sound impenetrable. If you try to invade China, it's pretty hard to get over that wall. You're going to have some difficulty.

Bun Cook certainly wasn't disagreeing. His praise for me continued to grow. "Bower is just reaching his peak," he told the Cleveland Plain Dealer. "Bower is every bit as good as Terry Sawchuk of Detroit. In fact, I'll say that right now, he compares favorably with Frankie Brimsek. He's the same type of goalie as Brimsek—a perfectionist."

It wasn't all bouquets for me that season. I suffered one of the most painful injuries of my career in a January 28, 1953 game at Pittsburgh. John McLellan, who'd later be my last coach in Toronto, fired one at me from 10 feet and it smacked me full in the mouth. The flesh was torn inside and outside of my mouth, as my teeth cut right through it. A four-tooth bridge was knocked out, a pivot tooth crumbled, a front bridge was destroyed, one anchor tooth was knocked out and another cracked. Another front tooth fractured at the gum line. It took 12 stitches to patch me up and plastic surgery in the summer to make me beautiful again. Dr. Philip Faix, who treated me, called it the worst injury to a goaltender that he'd ever seen. I'd lost eight teeth and taken 40 stitches to my face by this point in my career.

Nonetheless, I wanted to come back and finish the game, but I was overcome by dizziness from the loss of blood when I tried to return and Felix Perras, our standby goalie, was summoned to take over. I missed three games, but tried to look at it as a positive. I lost three pounds while I wasn't able to eat solid food and maybe that would make me faster. When I came back, I did so with this giant white bandage across my upper lip that resembled an oversized mustache.

One of the keys to our team was that we added Fred Glover in a trade with the Chicago Black Hawks. He'd won a Stanley Cup with the Detroit Red Wings in 1951-52 and boy he hated to lose. As a hockey player, he was one of the best competitors I'd ever seen. If you want to get an idea of how long I was in the minors, consider this—I was a teammate of the player who led the AHL in points during the 1940s (Fred Thurier), 1950s (Fred Glover) and 1960s (Willie Marshall).

Syracuse fell to us in the semi-finals, setting up our second Calder Cup final meeting with the Pittsburgh Hornets in three years. Once again, it was a sensational seven-game series. Pittsburgh beat us 4-3 in a four-overtime tilt in Game 6 to force the series to the limit. We battled through 60 minutes without a goal being scored, myself and Pittsburgh's Gil Mayer blocking everything thrown our way. It stayed that way until the 6:23 mark of the first overtime period, when our Bob Chrystal dented the twine and we were champions once more.

The rebuff by the NHL the year before was still gnawing at Jim Hendy's craw, so he came up with a new plan. He challenged the NHL to pit the Stanley Cup champions against us in a five-game series for the Legendary silver chalice. Naturally, the NHL scoffed at the notion, because they had nothing to gain from it and everything to lose. "The entire idea is purely a speculative venture," NHL president Clarence Campbell noted to the Cleveland News. "The Stanley Cup has always been emblematic of the world champions and therefore has been a trophy for major league clubs."

Cleveland would eventually get into the NHL in 1976, when the California Golden Seals relocated and were renamed the Cleveland Barons. I, on the other hand, wouldn't have to wait nearly as long.

CHAPTER THREE

MY BROADWAY DEBUT

Late in the 1952-53 season, rumors started to circulate that there was an NHL club interested in acquiring me from Cleveland. It turned out to be the New York Rangers. Carson Cooper, a former NHL forward who was scouting for the Rangers, kept showing up at our games. "Bower definitely belongs in the NHL," Cooper told the Cleveland News.

Apparently, the Rangers felt that Gump Worsley, who stood five-foot-seven and weighed only 145 pounds at the time, was too small to stand up to the pounding of being an NHL goalie.

Hearing the talk, I was starting to get a little bit excited. I guess I began to wonder several times while I toiled in the minors if I'd ever get a chance at the NHL. I was sure I was good enough and I knew my record was all right. But every year, there I was, back in Cleveland. I had heard the Barons were hanging on to me because they were trying to get into the NHL themselves and wanted me for their goalie if that happened. I liked Cleveland and they treated me fine there, but there's nothing like the big time.

Nothing happened until the summer. Then one day—it was July 20, 1953 to be precise—while I was working at the restaurant up in Waskesiu, I got a phone call from Cleveland general manager Jim Hendy. He'd made a deal and it was a big break for me. The Barons traded myself and Eldred Kobussen to the Rangers for Emile Francis and Neil Strain and an undisclosed amount of cash.

After I'd heard about the trade, as much as I wanted to see if I could make the grade as an National Hockey Leaguer, I was suddenly feeling mixed emotions. It's funny how that works. What's that old saying—be careful what you wish for? I didn't know whether I wanted to go or not because of my age, but it was something that I dreamed of my whole life, making the National Hockey League. Mr. Hendy called and he explained everything to me. "It's going to be rough up there for you," he said. "New York is a last-place club. You've got to work hard and do your best. They're developing their team."

Still, I was uncertain whether to make the move. I was going to be 29 in November and the restaurant was doing well. I thought about retiring. That's when the Rangers sent in the heavy artillery. They flew Muzz Patrick, who worked in the organization, out west to talk me into signing with them. He showed up in the restaurant one afternoon, right in the middle of the lunch rush. "We want you with the New York Rangers," he told me, but I didn't have time to talk. I was busy at the grill, flipping burgers. "Sit down," I told him, "and I'll make you some lunch." I cooked him up one of my signature burgers and after things died down, we sat and talked contract. He liked the taste of my cooking, I liked the sound of his figures. We came to a deal.

The Rangers were already expressing a lot of confidence in me. After the trade, Frank Boucher, their GM, was very complimentary in a Canadian Press article. "Bower goes about his game without flourishes," he said. "He rarely plays a bad game. In the last three years, injuries in goal have set the Rangers back. Now we have the goaltending depth to safeguard against possible injury."

To make the Rangers, I knew I'd have my work cut out for me. Even though they'd finished in fifth place the season before and hadn't made the playoffs since reaching the Stanley Cup finals in 1950, Worsley won the Calder Memorial Trophy as the NHL's best rookie in 1952-53. Maybe they were sour on him, but that's a pretty impressive piece of hardware to have on you resume.

Not long after the Rangers first acquired me, Gump came into Saskatoon for an appearance and ended staying and getting a job as a bartender. I heard he was bartending at one of the hotels. I went down to see him. I didn't tell him who I was. I didn't know whether he knew me, but I didn't think he did. So I came into the bar and he's serving beer and he kept looking at me like he was figuring, "I've seen that guy somewhere before." I looked at Gump and boy he was a chubby, little guy and I figured, "Boy am I going to get into shape and beat this guy out." Finally, when I was going I said, "Gumper, I'll probably be your standby come training camp." And he said, "I thought you were Johnny Bower. Well, the only thing I can say to you is good luck, because you've got your work cut out for you." Training camp opened that fall and here we were, ready to battle. Gumper, he was about five foot two, as pudgy as can be and here I am, as slim as can be. I had a strong camp and felt pretty good, but I was surprised when they said, "It's your job and not Gumper's." They farmed him out to Vancouver of the Western Hockey League, but before he left, Gumper said, "I'll come back and I'll get you."

The funny thing is, Gumper and I ended up being very good friends. We've been on a couple of cruises together. Gumper and his wife, they love to play cards. Every time we played against each other, when he was in New York and Montreal and I was in Toronto, when the game started, he'd wave to me and I'd wave to him, wishing good luck to each other, which was a nice gesture.

There were seven newcomers in the lineup when the Rangers opened the 1953-54 season—me in goal and a couple of other former Barons, Bob Chrystal and Ike Hildebrand. Ron Murphy, Max Bentley, Camille Henry and Billy Dea were the others and all but Bentley were rookies. Max was a grizzled veteran of 33, a two-time NHL scoring champ that we'd picked up from Toronto. Boy, he could sure handle that puck and skate and stickhandle. Camille Henry, who'd go on to win the Calder Memorial Trophy that season as the NHL's top rookie, he was one of the first to be adept at deflecting shots. He wasn't a very big kid, but I never saw anyone stand in front of a net and deflect shots like he could. He'd get a guy to shoot one from the point toward where he was standing and bingo, it was in the net.

One of the best things that happened to me in New York was that I got the chance to work with former Rangers goalie Charlie Rayner, who'd won the Hart Trophy as MVP of the NHL in 1949-50. Charlie was the one who helped me with my poke check. That was a lot of hard work, too. He said, "You can't handle the puck too well, can you? Well, you won't be here long if you don't learn how to handle it, if you don't know how to use the poke check." He showed me how after practice, boy he had a lot of patience with me, because it took me a lot of time to learn how to master it. I give him a lot of credit for that.

The poke check is a split-second decision, all timing. Just keep your eye on the puck and as soon as it comes close enough, you make your move. I knew when I could get them around the edge of that (face-off) circle, because I knew that's how far I could dive. You just had to watch that they didn't go the other way.

Charlie would go on the road scouting and I wouldn't see him for a couple of weeks. Then he'd come back and he'd ask me, "You still working on those angles I told you to use with the poke check?" Then he'd line six pucks up in front of the net and he'd have me dive for them. He'd watch me sometimes in the game and if he felt I should have poke checked the guy, even if he didn't score a goal, he'd come to me after the game and say, "John, you know that guy came pretty close to you, I told you, 'Don't forget to use that poke check.' Were you not concentrating? Were you afraid to do it?" I'd say, "I can't answer that. I'm not sure. The first thing in my mind was to stand up and wait for him." And Charlie would say, "But he cut right in front of the net. It's good thing the defenseman nailed him or they might have scored on you." And I said, "That's it, I rely on my defensemen." Then he said, "Well, don't rely on them too much. They tend to wander, you know."

After a while, the poke check came to me naturally. A lot of goaltenders today, they all seem to want to stay back in the net. New Jersey's Martin Brodeur is pretty good on the poke check and a couple of the Russian goalies are too, but most of the guys sit back and wait until the last second and then it's a giveaway completely that you're coming. You know yourself and if you practice it yourself, you know where the edge of the faceoff circles are in your own end. If you add your stick and put your arm out, you'll have somewhere between 52 inches and six feet, then you know that's as far as you can reach out. If they come in that range, then you've got him. Charlie would say to me so many times, "That guy was right inside that circle where you should have got him." Charlie was right.

That was probably one of my biggest assets, the poke check. Every goalie has got something. Brodeur's got that puckhandling ability where he can really headman the puck and so does Toronto's Ed Belfour. That's their big thing that they do and they really work at it. I've seen Belfour in practice stickhandling the puck around the ice. He'll wait patiently with the puck behind the net and draw in the other team's winger, then throw the pass up the other side of the ice. Now he's got a couple of guys caught up ice. Once in a while, he comes close to getting burned, but that's the chance you take. It's the same with the poke check. When you're guessing or you're fighting the puck, that's when everything goes wrong.

We opened on the road and my first NHL game came October 8, 1953 at Detroit's Olympia, where we lost 4-1 to the Red Wings. Red Kelly, who'd be my teammate on four Stanley Cup winners in Toronto, was the first to score on me in an NHL game. And of course, Gordie Howe, my summer fishing buddy from Waskesiu, he got one as well. Three days later, I bested Chicago 5-3 for my first NHL victory. "Our new goalie Johnny Bower, is every bit as good as Detroit's Terry Sawchuk," Boucher told The Hockey News. "He should have been in the league a couple of years ago."

I was finding my way around the NHL, but navigating New York was a different story. We opened at home October 25 against the Stanley Cup champion Montreal Canadiens. I was still staying in a hotel at the time. The hotel was next door to Madison Square Garden, but I walked out the wrong door. I got into a taxi and told him I was going to Madison Square Garden. The taxi driver told me, "Yeah sure. Hop in." He drove me around the block, made two right turns and I think I had to pay him a dollar and a half. After the game, I told the players I had to get a cab to the hotel. And one of the guys says, "To the hotel? It's right there behind us." I said, "You've got to be kidding me." I learned a lesson that day. The guys really teased me about that.

When I made it in New York, I was a little greedy. I thought, "Here I am in the National Hockey League. I'm going to have my name on the Stanley Cup someday." But I soon learned it wasn't going to happen in New York. We had some pretty good players in New York, it was just that the other teams were better than us. The other teams, like Toronto and Montreal, they were powerful. There was no way you could beat them. Every once in a while, you might get lucky and beat them or tie them, but the rest of the time, forget about it. We couldn't seem to do anything right to get into the playoffs. Gump Worsley, he'd been there so long and he couldn't get any playoff money until he got to Montreal. You'd ask him what team gave him the most trouble in the National Hockey League and he'd say, "The New York Rangers," his own team.

The New York papers referred to me as the "veteran rookie" of the Rangers and they also had some fun with me in the Rangers game program. "He hasn't lost a tooth since he's been with the Rangers," it noted. "That's because he keeps 'em in a glass in the dressing room." I'd lost nine of my teeth by this stage of my career.

We were stuck in fifth spot most of the season, just out of the playoffs. We caught Boston a couple of times for fourth place, the final playoff spot, but we couldn't get past the Bruins. In early January, Boucher, who was serving as coach-GM, handed the coaching reins to Muzz Patrick.

We seemed to get a spark from that, going 8-3-1 in our first 12 games under Muzz. I was also on a roll. In 22 games after January 1, 1954 I was 14-6-2 with a 2.14 goals-against average, including my first NHL shutout. I made 39 saves, 17 of them in the third period, as we won 2-0 in Chicago. It was a night of firsts. Glen Sonmor, my old Cleveland teammate, scored the winner and it was his first NHL goal. It was also the first NHL coaching victory for Muzz Patrick. We even won a game during that stretch at the Montreal Forum, a 2-1 decision on January 30 that was the first win there by the Rangers since April 6, 1950, a run of 24 games.

Beating Montreal was no mean feat, because the Habs were a powerhouse and they had Rocket Richard, the game's greatest goal scorer. I would say he was the toughest guy I ever played against.

The other goaltenders were scared of him, too. He'd never shoot in the same corner on me. On the ice, on the right side, up high on the left side, through your legs. He had such good wrists it made for a powerful wrist shot. He'd look at you and shoot in the same motion. I was lucky a lot of times. There were times I didn't even know I'd stopped him. I froze and he took the shot and he hit me dead on. He was waiting for me to move and I didn't. The rest of the time, he drove me up the wall. He was deadly. He had fire in his eyes. From the blue-line in he was probably the best player I ever played against. I used to go to church and light candles whenever I had to face the Rocket. The happiest day of my life was when he retired.

One night against the Canadiens, we iced the puck and that brought the faceoff back into our zone. Bill Chadwick was the referee. Here we are and I'm looking at the lineup they've got out and it's the Rocket on the right side and Jean Beliveau at center and Boom-Boom Geoffrion and Doug Harvey and I'm thinking, "Oh boy, have I got trouble."

Chadwick dropped the puck and it sort of rolled away from him so he didn't like it and blew the whistle to drop it over again. The Rocket left his position and said, "Johnny, you watch for number one." I didn't know what the Frenchman was talking about. I thought he was trying to break my concentration, but three minutes later, the Canadiens come down the ice and boom, the puck went in the net. I'm looking and it's the Rocket who scored the goal. Now I'm thinking about what he said and I shouldn't have been, because I was thinking about was that goal. A few minutes later, when the faceoff came back in our own end, Richard skated past me as fast as he could and said, "Johnny, now you watch for number two." In the second period, he got that second goal. And in the third period, with 15 seconds to go, he was at a bad angle, but I left the post and gave him an opening. Why I left that post I'll never know, but he banked the puck off the post and off my back and into the net. I see him skating toward me and he says, "Thank you for number three, Johnny."

Later on, we turned out to be pretty good friends. I did quite a few card shows with him over the years. He was a quiet person, but boy, oh boy, even when you talked to him he had that fire in his eyes. You had to be careful what you said to him. He looked like he might sock you one or something if he didn't like it. He was a great guy and a great competitor.

It was hard being a hockey player in the Big Apple. New York was a tough place to play. I think our biggest problem in New York was the coaching. They were always bringing in a new coach almost every year. They wouldn't keep one there too long. In the four years I was with the organization, they went through three coaches. After Muzz Patrick came a guy by the name of Phil Watson and boy was he tough. He'd drill you. That guy knew hockey, but he just didn't know how to handle men. We had some good players there, but I think we needed some good coaching. When you get a new coach every year, it's tough to play.

Another problem was the lack of practice time in our home rink. They had a place upstairs in Madison Square Garden and all the boards were made of steel. You wouldn't believe it. If we couldn't practice there, we used to go to the outskirts of town and there was an arena there where we'd practice. It was a tough situation there. They'd have basketball in the afternoon and they'd put the floor down over the ice. Then at night they'd have hockey. Or they'd have boxing in the afternoon and then hockey at night. Boy, the ice was really soft, the puck wouldn't slide much and the players were always complaining about it. But that's the way they ran the business.

They had great shows in there, big singers and comedians like Bob Hope. We were allowed to go and see the shows. Muzz Patrick at the time, said, "There's seats there if you want to go see them." When Phil Watson became the coach though, he didn't want us going to see the shows. We met some of the actors. The Dead End Kids used to come into the dressing room all the time, looking for free tickets from the players. There were quite a number of guys who came in the room. New York was known for that. The celebrities would come in the dressing room after the games, but the management didn't like that too much, especially if you'd lost the game.

The fans were pretty rough in New York and that's what I didn't like about it the most. It was different altogether in New York than what I found when I got to Toronto. New York people are different than Toronto people. Toronto, of course, it's a Canadian team and it's our national sport. They know their hockey in Toronto. New York was an entirely different story. They used to throw stuff on the ice when you let in a bad goal, they'd do a lot of stupid things there. If they could have gotten the chairs loose, they would have thrown them at you. They'd just boo you at any time, it seemed. They didn't know hockey, they didn't understand hockey. They knew more about the bad points than the good points, I guess. Sometimes, you didn't even want to play there. Sometimes, you'd wish you were back in the minors where you were more appreciated and people liked you.

In Toronto, you could walk down the street and they'd come up to you and say, "Hi, how are you?" They would look at you and say, "I know I've seen you somewhere before." And I'd say, "Are you a hockey fan?" And then they'd say, "I know who you are." It was a nice feeling. In New York, you could pass anybody and they never knew who you were. Gump Worsley used to tell me the same thing. I'd say, "Gumper, the fans here are sure different." "Sure they're different. It's not like Toronto or Montreal where they all know you. They're a different breed. They either like you or they don't like you, it's as simple as that. You'll find out as soon as you get on the ice."

Allan Stanley was one guy they didn't like. They were giving him a hard time every time he touched the puck. At one point, the team decided to only play him in road games. There were times there when he didn't know what to do with himself. It was hard on him, but he tried not to show it. I think he was probably one of the happiest guys in the world when he got out of New York. Why they didn't like Allan, I don't know. He was a good, steady defenseman who knew how to cut the angles for a goaltender. Sure he had his problems in turning and with guys going around him, but he knew how to steer them into the corner.

The worst night I had was when I'd allowed three goals in one period and I was bombarded with beer cans. Full beer cans. I had to crouch in the goal until the bombardment was over. For the most part, I was lucky, I guess, because at the end of the season, they voted me the most popular Ranger. The fans gave me a wristwatch and I sure was surprised when I got it! I still have it, but it doesn't run anymore.

Another great thing that happened for us in New York was that Nancy and I became parents for the first time. Our son Johnny was born March 11, 1954.

Try as we might, we just couldn't catch Boston and finished fifth, six points out of the playoffs, but I was being touted for both the Calder Trophy as rookie of the year and the Hart Trophy as MVP. I didn't win either, but it was nice to hear. I felt I'd had a good year in New York. I ended up with a 2.60 goals-against average for a fifth-place team and I thought that was a pretty good average. In fact, it was the lowest average posted by a Rangers goaltender in 14 years. And the 182 goals we surrendered that season would be the best total posted by the team until 1970-71. Even the Gumper tipped his hat to me. "Bower's a good goalie," he told The Hockey News. "I don't think there was much to choose between us in training camp. He got the call and he has done fine. He's been everything the Rangers expected."

I guess maybe all that talk went to my head, because when I went home, I was living high off the hog. I didn't work that summer. Usually, I worked hard all summer back in Prince Albert. I came to camp a little bit overweight and I was a little bit sluggish in training camp. I was about five or six pounds overweight and Gumper came into camp in pretty good shape. He had a better training camp than me. He got ahead of me and I couldn't catch him. They started off with Gump and I figured I'll get him again eventually, but I never did and I was back in the minors.

When I told Nancy that I was being sent back to the minors, she looked at me sadly and said, "How can they do that?" Sure, I was downcast when I was sent down—who wouldn't be—but not for long. I didn't like to be sent down, nobody does, but that's part of hockey. You don't get to spend the whole career in one place. The Vancouver Canucks were a New York Rangers farm club in the Western Hockey League and they sent me down there. It was sort of tough to play at first, after being in the NHL, but after about a week or so, once I got to know the players, it was all right.

I was in Vancouver for one season, but it turned out to be a good one. We finished third and I earned the award as the league's top goaltender with a 2.71 average, posted a league-leading seven shutouts, which tied a WHL record and was named to the Second All-Star Team. "Bower's been great," our coach Art Chapman told the Vancouver Province. "He's been the guts of our hockey club."

Going back down, I actually found that it was more difficult playing in the minors than in the NHL. That might not seem to make sense, because the better players are performing in the NHL, but I'll tell you why. It's because in the NHL, there was a pattern to the way the game was played. Systems were more set and players tended to play their positions, so a goalie got plenty of help. The minor leagues were more ragged. A goalie never knew what to expect. Some nights, you felt just like a duck in a shooting gallery. I got back to the NHL for a quick visit that season. The Gumper suffered a chipped bone in his ankle in a 2-2 tie November 21, 1954 at Toronto and I got the call to take over. We beat Boston 3-1 in my first start back in the bigs and tied the Bruins 2-2 the next night. After a 3-1 loss at Toronto, we stunned Montreal 4-1 at Madison Square Garden. I was 2-1-1 with a 1.75 goals-against average and there were rumblings that the Rangers spot might be mine once again. "It's Bower's job until further notice," Rangers coach Muzz Patrick told the Associated Press. But further notice came three days later, following a 6-1 loss to Detroit. When I got up the next day, there was a ticket for me to go back to Vancouver. Gumper was okay, Gumper was fine, they told me.

One good thing about being in the Western League was that Saskatoon had a team in the league, so my family got the chance to see me play. My father-in-law was not a well man at that particular time, so they didn't make it to many games, but they would listen to it on the radio. My family came down from Prince Albert to see me occasionally and I'd phone them from the hotel room and we'd go out for dinner.

Everyone remembers me as a Maple Leaf, but I also played goal for the Cleveland Barons and the New York Rangers before I got to Toronto.

I never learned to like giving up goals, but I was always willing to give the children a Merry Christmas as Santa Claus.

Several NHL greats posed for this photo. If you look closely, you'll pick out Bob Pulford, Bobby Hull, Red Storey and me, among others.

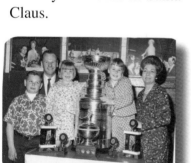

Nancy and I with our children John, Barbara, and Cindy surround the Stanley Cup.

Imagine how low my goals against average would have been if NHL nets were this small.

That's me behind the beard. I've frequently been cleverly disguised as Santa Claus at the Maple Leafs' annual Christmas party.

Those Richard brothers from the Montreal Canadiens—Maurice (the Rocket) and Henri (the Pocket Rocket)—were always a handful. Here, I'm foiling Henri close in on a breakaway.

The greatest joy of success is being able to share it with your family. Here I am riding through the streets of Toronto with my daughters Barbara and Cindy in the Maple Leafs' 1967 Stanley Cup parade.

We won four Stanley Cups while I was with Toronto, in 1962, 1963, 1964, and 1967. I also won the Vezina Trophy in 1960–61 and 1964–65.

The Leafs played in the Stanley Cup final in five of the first six seasons I was with the team.

Getting congratulations from my teammates after a 1965 victory over the Montreal Canadiens.

Thanks to my son John, Lord Stanley's mug has become my hat as we celebrate Toronto's 1967 Stanley Cup triumph in the Leafs's dressing room.

On many occasions following my 1970 retirement from the Leafs, I donned the pads and blocked shots during practice.

Checking out some junior prospects at Windsor Arena in 1981. After my retirement, I worked as a scout with the Leafs until 1990.

In January of 1980, when I was 55, the Leafs signed me to a $1 contract to serve as emergency goaltender for a game against Montreal. Luckily, Vincent Tremblay arrived from our Moncton, N.B. farm club in time to play the game and I didn't have to suit up.

The entire Bower clan gathered in Toronto for my 80th birthday party in 2004.

Nancy and I absolutely loved our life in Cleveland. Here we are in 2001, the night the Barons retired my No. 1 sweater.

I played goal for the Vernon, B.C. armed forces team. Many of the players in this photo were killed in the Allies' ill-fated 1942 raid on Dieppe, France during World War II.

An envelope from Bower Enterprises Inc., my own company.

That's me after I signed on with the Canadian Armed Forces during World War II. I was only 15 the first time I tried to enlist.

Nancy tending to one of the many wounds I suffered during my career from errant pucks.

Here I am in Vernon, B.C., where I went through basic training after enlisting in the Canadian army.

Bower's Big Boy was my restaurant and coffee shop in Waskesiu, Sask. It was the place to be in the summer months. They came from miles away for my world-famous burgers.

The luckiest day of my life. Nancy and I have just been married and as we left Cleveland's Trinity Church, my teammates used their sticks to provide an archway for the newly-weds to pass through.

Receiving my badge when the Peel (Ont.) Region Police Force named me their honorary chief.

These are the pads I wore when I played for the Vernon, B.C. armed forces team during World War II.

All decked out in my uniform when I was made an honorary police chief by Ontario's Peel Region Police Force.

This is it. The Real McCoy. My birth certificate. See, I've been telling the truth all along. It says I was born on Nov. 8, 1924.

Mr. Hockey, Gordie Howe and I lend a hand to a fan.

All decked out in my tuxedo the night I was inducted into the Canada Sports Hall of Fame.

It's amazing to me how many children who never saw me play a game still come up to me to talk.

Posing with the Stanley Cup. There's no greater feeling that a hockey player can have than to earn the right to lift Lord Stanley's mug.

Lifting the Stanley Cup with several of my Toronto teammates who earned it together four times, including Red Kelly, Bob Baun, and Allan Stanley.

The best thing that ever happened to me was meeting my wife Nancy. Here we are together during a break at my goaltending school.

I still get lots of fan mail and requests for autographs and do my best to answer all of the letters.

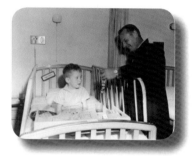

As athletes, we can make such a difference in the lives of the less fortunate. Here I am visiting a youngster in the hospital.

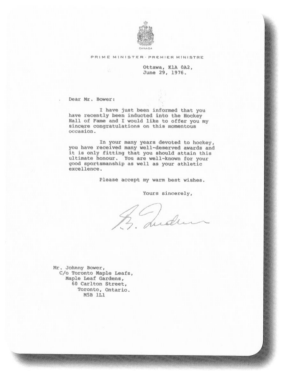

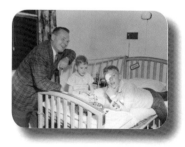

When you're a celebrity, a smile and a few minutes of your time can make the day of someone who is suffering, as I found out when I met these two excited youngsters during a hospital visit.

A congratulatory letter I received from Canadian Prime Minister Pierre Trudeau upon my induction into the Hockey Hall of Fame in 1976.

Talking to one of the many young goalies who passed through my Johnny Bower Goaltending School. Two of my more famous students were future NHLers John Vanbiesbrouck and Curtis Joseph.

Instructing the youngsters during my goalie clinic. I ran the school with my son John, my daughter Cindy, her husband Bruce and my grandsons John and Bruce for 20 years.

Fishing is one of my favorite passions. I hauled in these two beauties from Saskatchewan's Waskesiu Lake.

In 1960–61, my third year with the Leafs, I won the Vezina Trophy as the NHL's leading goaltender and was named to the NHL's First All-Star Team.

The best thing that happened in my hockey career was getting picked up by the Toronto Maple Leafs in 1958. I figured I'd be there a couple of years and ended up playing for the team until 1970.

Nancy and I chat with Mrs. Hockey, Colleen Howe. Gordie and Colleen are very good friends.

Nancy and I with Mr. Hockey and the Howe's business agent, Del Reddy at an All-Star game in Minnesota.

Four Hall of Famers in one foursome—Pierre Pilote, me, Mr. Hockey, and Marcel Dionne.

Gordie Howe and I chat with Hockey Night In Canada's Frank Selke Jr. moments after we'd beaten the Red Wings to win the 1962–63 Stanley Cup.

Chatting with Mr. Hockey, Gordie Howe and fellow Hall of Famer Clint Smith.

Gordie Howe and I spent many a summer's day coaxing the fish out of Waskesiu Lake in Saskatchewan and into our boat.

Pulling a puck that beat me out of the net. Nothing bothered me more than giving up a goal. As you can tell, the fans at Detroit's Olympia Stadium are enjoying this one far more than I did.

We battled Detroit five times in the playoffs, winning four of those series, including Stanley Cup final victories in 1963 and 1964. Here, I'm dumping Eddie Joyal of the Red Wings as Kent Douglas looks on.

Making a point-blank save on Normie Ullman of the Red Wings and Floyd Smith looks for a rebound.

A little advertising never hurts in getting the message out. An ad for my goalie school on the fender of a stock car.

Putting the kids through their paces at my goaltending school.

I've got the attention of these young hopefuls who attended my goalie school.

Going over a few pointers with one of my goalie school students. I always enjoy working with kids.

Nothing's more relaxing than an afternoon on the lake with my fishing rod in my hand.

Nancy's at the wheel and we're traveling in style in this fancy red sports car.

Sprawling to make a save. I posted 37 shutouts during my NHL career.

One of my summer jobs during my days with the Leafs was working for Borden Chemical, selling plastic film for wrapping meat and vegetables to grocery stores.

In my crouch, poised to handle the next shot. I played pro from 1945–70 and only wore a mask during my last two seasons.

Ron Ellis, my teammate on the 1967 Stanley Cup-winning Leafs club, meets with an avid fan.

How's this for a golf cart? Actually, the car and the poodle belong to Aldo Vettesse, a longtime business associate who runs my web site.

The Stanley Cup rests between a bevy of NHL stars, including: Lanny McDonald, Frank Mahovlich, Bill Gadsby, and Marcel Dionne.

I love to play golf. I participate in a number of charity tournaments each summer and can usually score around 92 or 93.

That's former Montreal Canadiens defenseman, Serge Savard, patting me on the back. Savard scored the final goal I ever allowed in the NHL, but just to show there's no hard feelings, every year, Nancy and I vacation at his El Senator Resort in Cayo Coco, Cuba. We're getting ready for the annual ball hockey game between some ex-NHLers and resort guests. As you can see, it's a well-attended event.

Talking things over with Leafs coach Punch Imlach. He was demanding, but he was also the best coach I ever played for.

Reliving the Montreal-Toronto rivalry with former Canadiens great Henri Richard. We beat Montreal for Toronto's last Stanley Cup title in 1967.

Maple Leaf Gardens, my home away from home for the 32 years that I worked for the Leafs.

Team photo of the 1977–78 Toronto Maple Leafs. I worked as a scout and goalie coach for the club from 1970–90.

An envelope with the official letterhead of the Toronto Maple Leafs. I looked forward to seeing these, because our paychecks came in them.

Answering questions from fans during an appearance at a Toronto area business.

Sharing a few laughs with some of the Maple Leafs oldtimers following a charity game.

No one shot the puck harder than Bobby Hull, Chicago's Golden Jet. Here, I'm safe, because he's only driving golf balls during a charity event where we appeared together.

I was part of a hockey legends promotion organized by Zeller's. Posing with me are fellow Hall of Famers Ted Lindsay, Stan Mikita, Maurice (Rocket) Richard, Rod Gilbert, and Frank Mahovlich.

I liked to come out of my net to play the puck. One of my unfulfilled hockey dreams was to score a goal.

Molson's Breweries depicted my likeness on beer cans, which was kind of ironic, because I've never been much of a beer drinker.

I remember this drive. It went straight down the middle of the fairway.

One stopper and four scorers. Wayne Gretzky, Glenn Anderson, Henri Richard, and Ted Lindsay join me at the 2000 NHL All-Star Game in Toronto.

Two Stanley Cup winners posing with Lord Stanley's mug. I won it four times with the Leafs and Nick Kypreos, the fellow on the left, he won the Cup in 1993–94 with the New York Rangers.

I admire many athletes in all sports. One of my favorites is pitcher Ferguson Jenkins, the only Canadian enshrined in baseball's Hall of Fame.

The 1964–65 Toronto Maple Leafs. We added Terry Sawchuk to share goaltending duties with me that season and we became the first NHL goalie tandem to share the Vezina Trophy.

A lot of people forget that I broke into the NHL with the New York Rangers. I played all 70 games for them in 1953–54 and my goals against average of 2.60 was the best posted by a Rangers goalie since 1940.

That's my likeness next to the Maple Leafs roster on a 1968–69 game program.

Bobby Baun was a stalwart on the Maple Leafs defense for all four of my Stanley Cup wins.

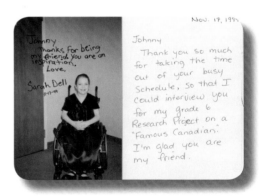

This young girl, Sarah Dell, interviewed me for her Grade 6 essay on famous Canadians.

We've just beaten Detroit to win the Stanley Cup in 1964 and we're all smiles.

The following season, the Rangers moved me back to the American Hockey League, assigning me to the Providence Reds. I was happy in Providence. At least down in Providence, the fans were good rabid fans. When I look back at the career that I had, I really can't complain about it. I was very lucky to be in some of the places that I ended up and with some of the teams that I played for. There were a lot of guys down in the minors that didn't have the players that I had in front of me. I was just very fortunate.

Our coach in Providence was a former Boston Bruins defenseman named Johnny Crawford. He was just like a father to us. He was a great hockey player in his day and a real good guy. One thing I remember, he never swore at the players. He always taught us to win, but he'd say, "If we win, we win and if we lose, we lose." He was just like one of the players. He'd played with Frankie Brimsek and was another who saw similarities between the two of us. "He's a ringer for Brimsek in the way he reacts, both on the ice and in the dressing room," Crawford told the Providence Journal. Terry Reardon, another former Bruin who was our GM, he was sort of strict, like most managers are. He was a good guy though, he was okay.

I'd enjoyed some wonderful years in the AHL with Cleveland and I was fortunate to be able to pick up right where I'd left off in Providence. We had a strong club there as well, finishing in first place and sweeping my old team, the Barons, in the Calder Cup final. I was named to the First All-Star Team and was completely stunned to learn that I'd won the Les Cunningham Trophy as the MVP of the AHL, the first goalie ever to win the award. "I say right now that Bower is the best in all pro hockey," Crawford told the Cleveland News. "That includes National Hockey Leaguers (Terry) Sawchuk, (Jacques) Plante, (Harry) Lumley and (Glenn) Hall."

One of the highlights about living in Providence was that the team was so often treated to wonderful meals by the Lamoriello family. I remember their son Lou, back then, he was just a little wee guy. But everybody knows him now. He had a sensational career as coach at Providence College, then topped that by taking over as GM of the New Jersey Devils and leading that team to three Stanley Cups. Back then, his father ran a restaurant, a fish shop and every time after a hockey game, we'd go down to their house and Lou's mom would put on some of the greatest meals you've ever seen. You wouldn't believe the food—spaghetti, chicken, steak, desserts—you name it. His dad had a little horse for Lou and our Johnny used to try and ride the horse.

That was one of the reasons I was so happy in Providence, because they were mostly Italian people. Boy oh boy, they'll do anything for you. They're wonderful people.

The 1956-57 season would be one filled with many milestones. We started the campaign by playing against the AHL All-Stars and made a little bit of history when we shut them out 4-0. It was the first time there'd ever been a shutout in a hockey all-star game at the professional level.

That launched us into another strong year. We finished on top of the standings again, I won my second Hap Holmes Memorial Award as the AHL's outstanding goalkeeper, repeated as the First All-Star Team goalie and shockingly, as league MVP. I was even named Rhode Island athlete of the year.

In January, Boston goalie Terry Sawchuk left the team, fighting illness and depression and there was talk that the Bruins were after me to replace him. But that's all it turned out to be, though, just talk. I did get back to the NHL briefly, filling in for an injured Gumper. He was out for about a week and I played a couple of games. I lost the first game and then I lost the second game, then they sent me right back to Providence. Reardon didn't think I had anything to worry about. He was certain my time would come again. "He can't miss returning to the big league." our GM told the Providence Journal.

A 6-0 shutout of Springfield was my 36th in AHL competition, tying me with Nick Damore for the AHL career mark. On March 10, 1957, I blanked Rochester 8-0 and the record was mine. I'll tell you, the final minute of that game, it was the longest minute of my life. I thought the last 60 seconds would never end. By the end of the season, I'd played 528 AHL games, one off the record for goalies held by Harvey Bennett. The only downer that season was that we were eliminated from the playoffs by Rochester in the semi-finals.

I headed back to Saskatchewan that summer very content with my hockey lot in life. But believe it or not, it was about to get better. And I had Marcel Paille to thank for that. Paille had finished the 1956-57 season as Cleveland's goaltender. But the Rangers, who owned his NHL rights, wanted to assign him to another AHL club for the 1957-58 campaign. That's when Cleveland GM Jim Hendy pointed out a clause in Paille's contract which stated that he could only play in the AHL for Cleveland. So the Rangers made him an offer. They said, "How about we give you Bower, then?" Well, that was an offer Mr. Hendy couldn't refuse. He didn't wait long to make the move, sending Ed MacQueen and cash to the Rangers for me. I was going back home.

It was a surprise to me when they got me back again. When I found that out is when I went back to Cleveland, I was very happy. The Barons signed me to a contract with a no-trade clause. When I got back to Cleveland, I had another strong season there. We finished second in the standings, I won the Hap Holmes Award again, was once more a First All-Star selection and became the first three-time MVP in the history of the AHL.

I even wiped a 17-year-old record off the AHL books. It started when we tied Buffalo 2-2 November 27, 1957. Dick Gamble beat me with Buffalo's second goal at 15:09 of the third period. I kept the slate clean the rest of the way, including a 10-minute overtime period, then posted 24 saves in a 1-0 OT win over Hershey. A 36-save performance in a 2-0 victory over Springfield followed, then a 9-0 whitewash of Hershey that required just 23 saves from me. The shutout sequence finally ended at 8:26 of the second period December 7, 1957, when Lou Jankowski scored on me in our 6-2 win over Buffalo. All tallied up, I'd gone 249:51 without allowing a goal, wiping out the mark of 221:02 established by Hershey's Nick Damore in 1939-40. It was a great one for the team. The players had bonuses for goals for and goals against, both the forwards and the defensemen, so we all worked together. And I'd get $10 a shutout. They haven't broken that record yet. Every year, I expect I'll get the call to tell me that they've broken Bower's shutout record, but it's still holding true. That's nice, but records are made to be broken, so if they break it, they break it. I've held it for a long time, so maybe it's time for somebody else to get it.

Boy, those were good years. Experience was starting to swell in me. I'd been in the minors a long time and once you get that experience, you start to get better and better and you've got that confidence in yourself. I had very successful teams in front of me and that made a big difference. There was another momentous occasion for the Bowers that season. Our daughter Cindy was born on Jan. 11, 1958 in Cleveland. Nancy and I were now the proud parents of two children.

Late in the season on March 9, we were playing my old team, Providence, and I was headed toward my ninth shutout of the season, which would have been a new AHL single-season record. Jimmy Bartlett was one of the roughest and toughest guys playing for Providence and he was coming down the wing. He was a great skater and he was moving kind of quickly, headed for the goal net, when he sort of got tripped up from behind. At that time, the nets didn't dislodge very easily, so the goalies would usually stop the guys to keep them from getting hurt, no matter how bad of a guy he might be. I threw my body in front of him and my belly pad got caught and moved and when he crashed into me, he fractured three of my ribs. Our trainer Jim Boag had to come in to finish the game.

I'd rather have 20 stitches in the face than one sore rib. With those facial cuts, you could still get in there and play, but with broken ribs, I was done for the season. The Barons brought in Lucien Dechene from Saskatoon of the Western League and he played the rest of the way as Cleveland was upset by Punch Imlach's Springfield Indians in the playoffs.

It was a disappointing way for my season to end, but overall, I couldn't have been happier to be back in Cleveland. I knew that I was getting older, 33, which was pretty old to be a hockey player at that time. I wanted to stay in Cleveland. I was going to retire in Cleveland.

I figured my days were pretty well over as far as the National Hockey League was concerned. I shouldn't say I didn't care, because I still wanted to have my name engraved on the Stanley Cup. I just felt that my chance had come and gone. But I was about to discover the NHL held a different opinion.

CHAPTER FOUR

A RELUCTANT LEAF

During the 1957-58 season, Bob Davidson, who was chief scout for the Toronto Maple Leafs, began bird-dogging our games in Cleveland. I soon found out I was the object of their affection. Both the Leafs and Boston tried to make deals for me during the season, but I held veto power with a no-trade clause in my contract and I refused to go. I had no desire to leave Cleveland.

The Leafs weren't going to take no for answer. On June 3, 1958, they selected me from Cleveland in the intra-league draft. I really didn't want to go. I thought, "Oh my gosh, I'm 33 years old." I thought there was no way I could help. Davidson said, "Johnny, we're going to be honest with you. We just want you for a couple of years, that's all. After that, if things go well for you, we'll give you a job as a goaltender coach." I still didn't know. I told Jim Hendy, our GM in Cleveland, "I don't think I'd like to go." He said, "You don't?" and I said, "No." He said, "Well, I'll tell you, if you don't go, you'll get suspended." And I said, "Suspended from what?" And he said, "Suspended from hockey. You won't be able to play. So I'll tell you what I'll do. I'll put a clause in the contract stating that if you do not make it in Toronto, you come back to Cleveland." I thought, "Oh that would be great" and that's what really pushed me to go to Toronto.

Mr. Hendy helped me put together my demands to present to the Leafs. I asked first of all for the clause that I could only be sent down to Cleveland. I sought a two-year contract at $10,000 per season that stated that even if I was injured during training camp that fall, my contract would still be paid in full to me. I also asked that the Leafs pick up the tab for all of my moving expenses. Mr. Hendy presented Billy Reay, the Leafs coach, with a photostat copy of my contract demands.

Even after I presented them with my wishes, I was still reluctant about making the move. There were so many young goaltenders around, why the Leafs chose me I don't know. I wanted to stay in Cleveland. There was a big company there, Thompson Products, which made car parts and if you wanted a job for the summer, you worked at Thompson Products. Being a hockey player, jobs came very easily for me. As it turned out, though, it was my summer job in Waskesiu which finally convinced me to give Toronto a try.

Mr. Hendy told me to look at things from a practical point of view. "If you're not thinking in terms of hockey, think in terms of hamburger," he said, referring to my Bower's Big Boy restaurant. "You're selling the best hamburgers west of Winnipeg right now, but who knows about it except ourselves? But if you make it with the Leafs, everybody in Canada will know that your burgers are every bit as good as your goaltending. You won't be able to fry the things fast enough." That just about did it. Then Punch Imlach, who'd just been named assistant GM of the Maple Leafs, visited me in Saskatoon and we finalized the deal. I was going to Toronto.

When I got to training camp in the fall of 1958, there must have been eight goaltenders, but I was so far ahead of all of them. Not that I'm bragging, but I mean these guys they had in camp, they were really lacking in experience. They were mostly kids just up from junior hockey and of course I had a jump on them because I had all that experience from playing in the minor leagues. Every time I played in an exhibition game or in scrimmages, I was doing really great. "Johnny Bower is the best goaltender we've had in 20 years," Leafs owner Stafford Smythe boasted in the Toronto papers. Things went pretty well in training camp and Billy Reay came in and said, "Hey John, you made it." So I signed a contract with them.

The Leafs hadn't made the playoffs the previous two seasons and hadn't won a playoff series since capturing the Stanley Cup in 1950-51, so I was one of eight newcomers who made the team that fall. "Bower will give us a big lift in goal," Reay told the Toronto Star's Red Burnett. "He's a great clutch player and uses his stick more effectively than any goalie I've seen in years. It's amazing the way he can intercept passouts and poke that puck off an attacker's stick. He's also very good at cutting down the angles and what's more important, he's an experienced pro who is at his best in a tight spot."

When I first got to Toronto, I met Turk Broda, who'd won four Stanley Cups as the Leafs' goalie and he said, "Johnny, let me tell you, the fans in Toronto are great. If you play your heart out and you work hard, they'll appreciate you. They're going to give you No. 1 to wear and don't you ever let anyone take it off your back." That was great advice.

The plan was for the Leafs to carry both myself and Ed Chadwick, who'd been their No. 1 goalie the previous two seasons, leading the NHL in games and minutes played both seasons. Eddie was 25 at the time, eight years younger than me, but he accepted me like a long lost brother. We were rivals for a position, but there was no bitterness whatsoever. I wanted to help Eddie in any way I could and he felt the same way toward me. The way I looked at things, he had a future and I had a past, but I guess the Leafs felt differently, because I got the nod to start on opening night, October 11,

1958 at Maple Leaf Gardens against the Chicago Black Hawks.

Let me tell you, I was nervous that night. I looked down the other end of the ice and saw Bobby Hull and Stan Mikita and all the big guys and I thought, "Oh man." I was pretty shaky at the start, but we came out of the opening period ahead 1-0. George Armstrong, our captain, came in after the first period and said, "You've got to settle down." I said, "I'll be okay," and as the game progressed, I was fine. But that first shot, it just about killed me. If you let that first shot in, for some reason, the roof falls in and you start to fight the puck. Tod Sloan, a former Leaf and my ex-teammate in Cleveland, he scored a pair of power-play goals on me and Hull also scored as we lost 3-1.

We lost our next game 5-2 at Chicago and also fell 4-3 in Montreal before I finally tasted victory as a Maple Leaf, defeating Boston 3-2 October 18 at Maple Leaf Gardens. But then we dropped a 3-1 decision the next night at Detroit and were off to a dismal 1-4 start. It was made clear to us that this was completely unacceptable. "If there were no protected list and we didn't have to get waivers before sending players down, at least three of these guys would be on their way to Rochester," Imlach told Red Burnett of the Toronto Star.

That's the way the game worked back then. It was an up and down situation. When I was with Cleveland, if you were playing for GM Hap Day in Toronto and he didn't like you, he'd send you right down to Pittsburgh. Three-quarters of that Toronto team was sent down and we had to play against them in Cleveland. George Armstrong used to tell me Day had a pocketful of tickets for Pittsburgh. Everybody had a fling in Pittsburgh and they'd play their heart out to get back to Toronto. It was the same with Montreal. If you didn't play the way coach Toe Blake wanted you to play, you were sent down. Tough luck. You'd ride the buses back and forth down in the minors.

One move the Leafs decided to make was in net, where Chadwick took over for me. I was pretty shaky at first and I was fighting the puck for a long time. I was also fighting for a job with Eddie and to me, he was a doggone good goaltender. I had a tough time trying to beat him out. They just started to alternate us. Punch said, "Whoever plays better, that's who's going to play."

Things continued to be inconsistent for us and it cost Billy Reay his job. First, Punch was promoted to GM on November 21 and eight days later, he fired Reay. At first, it looked like Alf Pike was going to be brought in as coach, but Punch opted to take the reins himself.

I didn't know for a while whether I was going to stay up or not. There were rumors I was going to be placed on waivers or traded. I was pretty scared for awhile, but they had a lot of confidence in me. When Punch took over the team, I had a good, long talk with him. He said, "I don't care how old you are, as long as you play the way I tell you to play and not the way you know how to play. Do like I've told all the other players, and we'll be successful" and he was right. We listened to him and whether we thought he was doing things wrong, it didn't matter. Most of us didn't think he was doing things wrong, but there were a few guys who didn't like him.

One of the first things Punch did when he took over was to give each player a copy of "The Power of Positive Thinking" by Dr. Norman Vincent Peale. He signed my book, "Best of luck, Johnny. I know you can do it." I read that book from cover to cover on the bus, on the train and at home. In fact, I read it twice. I began to believe that I was every bit as good as Terry Sawchuk, Glenn Hall and Charlie Rayner. Finally, I started to get used to the guys and the teams I played against. I started to find myself, to have more confidence in myself. That's when the good things started for me.

When March, the last month of the regular season, rolled around, we were in last place. I played five straight games to begin the month 2-2-1 as we quit the cellar. Eddie took over for a 6-2 loss to Montreal March 11, then Punch decided to ride me the rest of the way. And what a ride it was. We were seven points behind the New York Rangers for the final playoff spot with five games to play.

I couldn't believe that we were going to get in the playoffs, but Punch always stressed during the run that we were going to make it. "We're going to get in the playoffs," he'd say. "I know we're going to get in. You guys can do it if you want to do it. Put your heart and soul into it and you'll make it." Everybody tried their darnedest, but once you get seven points behind with five games left, it's pretty hard to catch up. But we started off on the right foot, taking a weekend home-and-home set with the Rangers by 5-0 and 6-5 counts. Now the deficit was three points. We won 6-3 at Montreal and beat Chicago 5-4 and were one point back of New York with one game to play. It was a tough stretch there and it had come right down to the wire. We were in Detroit and we were losing and all of a sudden we ended up winning the game 6-4 on third-period goals by Dick Duff and Billy Harris. Then Montreal went out and beat the Rangers 4-2, so we were in. That was really something. I think everybody went to church there. I don't think we thought we were going to get in at all. But we got in and it certainly paid off.

Boston would be our first-round playoff opponents. After 14 years as a pro, I was going to finally experience the Stanley Cup playoffs and if I thought I was tense before that first regular-season game in Toronto, the pressure was about to get ratcheted way up.

I was really nervous because there was a lot on the line. When you're playing in the playoffs, your first game, you get pretty shaky there for awhile. And it showed. Boston whipped us 5-1 in the opener and followed up with a 4-2 decision in Game 2. Then George Armstrong, my roomie, steadied me down quite a bit. He said, "Don't worry about it. If you let in a bad goal, we'll get it back for you." He gave me the confidence that I needed. Being a goaltender, you have to have confidence in yourself and in some of the players, knowing that they'll help you out.

It sure made a difference in Game 3 when we got back on home ice. We were 3-2 winners, my first-ever Stanley Cup victory coming when Gerry Ehman scored at 5:02 of overtime. We worked overtime again in Game 4 and I made a save in the extra session that people still talk about as the turning point in the series. I got caught out of position a little bit and Boston's Vic Stasiuk had me at his mercy. I was on one side of the net and I had to get over really quickly. I'd lost my stick, so the only things I had to get in the way of the puck were my head and my hands. People sitting behind my net were so sure it was over, they started putting on their coats and hats. But I dove across and Stasiuk's shot glanced off my glove and then hit my forehead. It didn't cut me or anything, but if I didn't do that, we would have lost for sure. I was very lucky to stop it. And even luckier when Frank Mahovlich scored a few minutes later to give us another 3-2 victory.

I remember after that game, my son John threw his arms around me, gave me a hug and said, "Daddy's just won the Allan Stanley Cup." We tried to explain to him that we were playing for Lord Stanley's Cup, but he was only five years old and convinced that Allan Stanley, my teammate in New York who'd also landed in Toronto, was the one who donated the trophy.

We split the next two games and it all came down to Game 7. Boston led 2-1 after two periods on Leo Boivin's go-ahead tally, but we rallied once more. Bob Pulford tied it and Ehman potted the series winner with 2:33 left in regulation time. We were down and we came back to win. When you win like that, then you figure you're on your way for the next series.

Then we got to Montreal and boy, did the Canadiens have other ideas. We did the best we could, but they had a powerhouse squad there. They had guys like Jacques Plante in goal, who was in his prime, playing great hockey and Doug Harvey anchoring the defense. Up front, there was Jean Beliveau, the Rocket and Dickie Moore. They were just two steps ahead of us, a lot better than we were.

We carried them to five games, though. That wasn't too bad. Duff's overtime goal won us the third game 3-2 on home ice and what a great competitor Dickie Duff was. To me, for his size, he was tough. He just wanted to play and play and play. There's a fellow who should be in the Hockey Hall of Fame. Why they don't put him in, I just don't know. If you check his record, he's got close to 300 goals and he won about six Stanley Cups. He doesn't know why they won't put him in. We've written letters giving them the reasons why we feel he should be in there. As far as I'm concerned and a lot of other players who played in our time are concerned, we feel that Dickie Duff should have been in there a long time ago.

Coming to camp for the 1959-60 season, I had a good feeling about our team and about myself. I now felt that I belonged in the NHL and that did my mental state a world of good. It's funny that people viewed me as calm, cool and collected, because I sure had them fooled. I was a worry wart. I worried mostly about the goals that were scored against me. A lot of times, if I didn't stop them, I'd let the team down and that bothered me a lot. I had trouble sleeping at night after a game. I couldn't get to sleep until three or four o'clock some nights, thinking about mistakes I made. My roomie George Armstrong would go crazy because I kept him awake so much. It was just one of those things. You worked so hard in practice, I didn't want to give up anything. I'd even get nervous when I'd give up five or six goals in practice.

I was pretty quiet on game day. I was a loner, so I would be pretty quiet. I thought a lot about the game on game day. Even when Nancy drove me to the rink, I didn't say too much. She'd just say, "Good luck to you and have a good game" and that was about it. At least I wasn't nervous like Glenn Hall and those goaltenders who get upset stomachs.

A lot of times, I felt really good in the warmup and I thought before we played, "I'm going to have a good game" and then I'd go out and play some of my worst games. Why, I don't know what it was. I can't explain it to this day. It was just something that would come over me. I'd feel like a million bucks and I'd play terribly. Then there were times when I felt kind of lackadaisical in my pre-game preparations and I'd come up with a big game.

In New York and don't get me wrong, I'm not saying the players weren't any good, but there just was a different feeling to training camp with the Leafs. I don't know what it was, whether the players didn't care or what, but in Toronto, it was different. Montreal had won more Stanley Cups than Toronto and the Leafs didn't like that. In Toronto, they'd tell you that you had to play in training camp like you played in the game. That's the way you learn and the way you have to play. When Punch got there, he said, "We're going to practice, practice, practice, until we learn." That's the way we learned to be successful.

The fans in Toronto were great. Oh sure, I got booed one or two nights because I'd played lousy, but that's their prerogative. There wasn't going to be much reason to boo for the next several years, though. We beat Chicago 6-3 in our home opener, the first time the Leafs had won the first game at Maple Leaf Gardens in four years. We were playing with much more cohesion than the season before and it showed. Punch predicted we'd pull down between 70-75 points.

I'd won the No. 1 job in net. There'd be no more sharing. Ed Chadwick played just four games during the season and spent most of the time in Rochester. At the end of the 1960-61 season, the Leafs traded him to Boston for Don Simmons, which caught me by surprise. You know, Ed Chadwick wasn't a bad goalkeeper. I checked his record and he's not a bad goaltender. Why they let Ed Chadwick go I have no idea. They had a lot of goalkeepers in Toronto at that time, but Ed played really well for Toronto, even after I got there, but the next year he was gone. To this day, it's a mystery. He played some good games for Toronto and he was a lot younger than I was.

We were in third place at mid-season, then in February, Punch pulled off one of the best trades he ever made. Detroit defenseman Red Kelly had been dealt by the Wings to the

New York Rangers, but opted not to go and retired, voiding the move. But Punch started talking to the Wings and a few days later, we got Kelly from Detroit for defenseman Marc Reaume. Kelly had won the Norris Trophy in 1954 and was one of the NHL's best defensemen, but the biggest surprise of all was when Punch said that Kelly was going to play center.

Punch always said, "If I can get three strong centermen down the middle, I can win the Stanley Cup." And he would. He had Bobby Pulford, who was a great centerman and now he had Kelly. When they moved Kelly to center, it caught everyone by surprise. But it made sense, because Kelly was great defensively and a marvel at passing the puck. He was one guy who could put the puck on your stick. He didn't slap it, just shot it smoothly and followed through, just like a golfer's swing. He had to keep his head up though when Eddie Shack was on his line, because they had a few collisions in those days.

Punch liked to acquire veterans with playoff savvy and one of those guys was Bert Olmstead, who we got from Montreal. We used to have some good meetings with Bert. He was more or less Punch's assistant. George Armstrong, our captain, would say his piece and then Bert would get up and say, "Look, I'm not used to losing. I came from a hockey team where we were taught to win, win, win." And that's why they were so successful. They were taught that by Toe Blake, to never mind losing. Bert was a great competitor. I remember one time, Bert came up to me. "I'm going to tell you something, John," he said. "I'm not the greatest skater in the world, but when I go down that wing and I get caught, you better not let any goals in on my side of the ice." He played with George Armstrong, my roomie, so what am I going to do? All of the goals are going in on George's side of the ice. That's the kind of competitor Bert was. When the season was all over, he'd go straight back to Scepter, just outside of Saskatoon, where he had a farm and work on the crops.

Another interesting character who was part of my first Leafs teams was Gerry James. He also played for several years with the Winnipeg Blue Bombers and won the Grey Cup with them. We called him Jesse and for a couple of years he came up with Toronto. In 1959-60, he played on an agitating line with Garry Edmundson and Johnny Wilson. For a football player, he wasn't a bad hockey player. He was a good guy to have on the hockey club. He was strong, but he used to duck a lot. Guys were getting crippled because he would duck and they would fly right over him. I guess that's the way it was in football. He was so used to it, to duck and get out of the way.

We finished the season in second place, with 79 points, the club's best finish since 1950-51 and better than Punch had predicted. We beat Detroit in a six-game semifinal and I even held my good friend and old nemesis Gordie Howe to one goal over the course of the six games. "If Johnny Bower continues to give them that fantastic goaltending, Maple Leafs could go all the way," Detroit GM Jack Adams expressed to the Toronto Star.

We met the Canadiens once more for the Stanley Cup and they were too much for us again. This time, they swept us aside in four games. Montreal didn't lose a playoff game, going 8-0 to win the Stanley Cup for the fifth successive season. I would say that those Montreal teams were the best I ever saw. Imagine what it was like for a goaltender to face Jean Beliveau, Doug Harvey, the Richard brothers, Henri and the Rocket and Bernie Geoffrion and you'll understand how it felt to be me that spring.

We returned to our summer home in Saskatoon and a few weeks after the finals ended, our family grew again when Nancy gave birth to our daughter Barbara on May 23, 1960. We now were parents of three children and as is often the case with hockey players, each child was born in a different city—John in New York, Cindy in Cleveland and Barbara in Saskatoon.

We were all looking to once more take that next step when the 1960-61 season rolled around and a couple of newcomers figured to be part of the plan. One was right-winger Bob Nevin, who'd had a couple of brief stints with us in previous seasons, but this year he finally made the grade for good. Bobby Nevin was a real great guy, always smiling, a happy go lucky guy. He was a great checker, always up and down the wing and a good penalty killer. He'd get his share of goals, too. And what a great competitor, I was glad he was on our side.

The other rookie was Dave Keon, up from one of our junior clubs, St. Mike's. He was a great skater, a great faceoff man and checker, who scored his fair share of goals and gave us that third solid center that Punch wanted. He was absolutely loved by the people. Davie wasn't what you'd call a hitter. He was a nice playmaker. He killed penalties, he scored goals and was very good at getting faceoffs, particularly in our end which is so important. I must admit I was surprised when the Leafs named him captain in 1969. I didn't think he was going to be a captain. I didn't think that Davie had it in him to be a captain. He was captain for a few years there and did a good job from what I understand, until he decided to go to the WHA in 1975. To me, he was so quiet in the dressing room. Of course, George Armstrong could be quiet at times, too. All these quiet guys, they're the ones you've got to watch.

We were going like gangbusters that season, even challenging Montreal for first place in the standings. Frank Mahovlich was enjoying a career year and had scored 26 goals in our first 29 games, finishing the season with a club-record 48 tallies. Frank had a great year. He came so close to 50 goals. You know, Punch thought he was a lazy hockey player, but what Punch didn't realize was that Frank had that long stride. He looked like he wasn't moving, but he really was. Keon was on his way to the Calder as the NHL's top rookie and the old guy in net was also headed for an award-winning campaign.

We'd gone 14 in a row without a loss when we played in Detroit on February 12. Howie Young, who was one of the NHL's toughest players, he came down the ice and barreled right into me, bowling me over. My legs twisted underneath me and I knew immediately that something was wrong. But the strange thing was that I played a lot better after I was hurt. Alex Delvecchio got a breakaway a few minutes later and I stopped him. The thing is, I couldn't move. He wanted me to move, but I couldn't and he hit me. I was lucky there. They took me to hospital after the game and it was determined I'd suffered a torn left hamstring. After that, I was finished. I came back to Toronto. They sent me to hospital and I was there for a week. Gerry McNamara and Cesare Maniago took over in goal and I have to tell you, they did a great job. We were leading the Vezina Trophy race when I was injured and they maintained our advantage.

That was one of the greatest thrills I've ever had, winning the Vezina Trophy in 1961. Sometimes, I still can't believe it. They gave me a lot of credit, but the team really played well in front of me. It's something I wouldn't say I never dreamed of winning it, because I knew I had good players in front of me, but to win it, what a thrill! It's so hard to explain, I just about cried my head off. I remember the trophy presentation vividly. It was before the game. Back then, all the ceremonies were held before the game. NHL president Clarence Campbell wouldn't wait until after the game. There was no way.

There was a tragic note that took a bit of the luster off the Vezina win. A few days before I clinched the trophy, Jim Hendy, my good friend and former GM in Cleveland, died. I admired him. He was just like a father to me. He was so good, not only to me and my family, but to the whole team. When he passed away, I was really sorry to see that. Joe Lamantia, who used to be the timekeeper at Maple Leaf Gardens, he took a plane with me to Cleveland to pay our respects. He was a great hockey man and everybody loved Jim Hendy.

The return trip was pretty rough, I thought for a while we were going to join Mr. Hendy. It was a small plane and we hit some turbulence. Joe got so nervous, I've never been hugged so hard in my life. I told him, "Get back in your own seat." We all had white knuckles, but when it was all over, everything turned out okay.

Another thing I didn't enjoy that season was the rehabilitation sessions following my injury. They weren't exactly the high tech drills the players enjoy today. Punch said when you're injured, you have to keep working out, even when the team was on the road. I used to go out with the Toronto Marlboros junior team and practice with them when I was hurt. On Sundays, Stafford Smythe used to come on the ice, all of the kids and a lot of the family members of the owners of the Leafs would come on the ice and shoot pucks at me. Some of them couldn't control their shots so I'd have to do a little bit of ducking. Tommy Smythe, Stafford's son, wasn't a bad little hockey player. Harold Ballard's boys would be out there and they could shoot it pretty good, too. We'd pick sides, usually the Ballards versus the Smythes. If one side got too far ahead, I'd switch ends and play for the other team. You were just getting on the ice, trying to get the feel of things again.

Another tradition I started back then was waving to Nancy's mom when I was picked as one of the game's three stars. She said to me, "It would be very nice of you when you do get picked as a star to wave to me." I said, "Okay, I'll do that, mother." The first opportunity I got, I waved and everybody thought I was waving to all of the mothers, but it was for her. She was the one who started it. When I got back to Saskatoon, she said, "Well it's about time you realized that you should wave to me." And I said, "Well, I did it" and she said, "Yes, you did. It was very, very nice of you to do that."

We met Detroit in the first round of the playoffs for the second spring in a row, but this time, things didn't go our way. Even though we'd finished 24 points ahead of the Wings, we opened the playoffs with both myself and defenseman Bob Baun out injured, then Olmstead got hurt during Game 1 of the series. Maniago played the first two games, then I tried to come back, but I was rusty and wasn't

100 per cent. Meanwhile, at the other end, Terry Sawchuk was outstanding and they took us out in six games.

I think when you lose like that, it is sort of a letdown. Everybody felt pretty bad, but my attitude always was we got beat out by a better club and that's it and then you look ahead to next season. That's hockey for you. It's tough when you lose something like that, but you have to forget it and move on. It's water over the dam. Besides, we'd find out soon enough that the best was yet to come.

CHAPTER FIVE

ARMY AND ME

My life has been influenced significantly by two armies. One was the Canadian Armed Forces, with which I served during World War II. The other Army continues to impact my life today, as he has done for nearly a half century.

That would be George Armstrong.

Army, as we all know the former captain of the Toronto Maple Leafs, was my roommate for the majority of my 12 seasons with the team. He's also my closest friend and more often than not, the guy who can get my goat better than anyone.

I like to tell George that I was the one who got him to the National Hockey League. He was sent down to Pittsburgh of the American Hockey League during the 1951-52 season and he scored a hat-trick on me, but he never did touch the puck. When I got to Toronto, I said to him, "Do you remember that?" One shot hit one of my defensemen and went in. He was standing there and he put his stick up in the air and they gave him the goal. The other one was a screen shot and he put his stick up again and they gave it to him. The third one was a tip in. The next day, he was back with Toronto in the National Hockey League for good, so I tell him I put him there.

I roomed with him for 10 years. We shared a lot of great times and a lot of sad moments because of games that didn't go our way. When I got to Leafs camp in the fall of 1958, he was my first roomie and Chief said, "I don't know why every training camp I have to room with a goaltender? I had other goaltenders before you came." I said, "I don't know why I got you, either? I was surprised that I got you. I was hoping I'd get a good roomie." Neither of us knew whether the arrangement would be permanent. "We'll just have to wait and see," he said. "I don't know how the list is going to be made out." For a little while in training camp, they took him out of my room and gave me Gerry Cheevers, because they wanted me to work with him. When we moved Gerry, when the season started, I went back with Chief. I said, "Did you ask for me?" and he said "No. I don't like you at all. You're a white man and I'm an Indian." And he kept going on, moaning like that. He's a colorful guy, the Chief. We called him the Chief because of his Native Canadian heritage. George's mom was of Iroquois descent.

George is an easy guy to talk to and he's a lot of fun, a really easy guy to get along with. Off the ice, I had a lot of fun with him. We could talk about different things. He doesn't have a bad word for anybody. The only person he ever had a bad word for was himself. He would criticize himself more than anyone else.

On the road, we'd go for walks and window shopping, stuff like that. We'd go to a show the odd time here or there. We'd go out and he wouldn't drink. He'd have a Shirley Temple. That's a strawberry drink, a woman's beverage, but that's all he would order. He was just like a brother to me, more or less. To this day, he always carries a little pocket knife with him and he'd say, "You know, we have to be blood brothers." Then he'd draw out the knife and I'd say,

"Well, what do you do?" And he said, "You take your hand out and extend your wrist. I'm going to put a little incision on your wrist and then I'm going to put one on mine and we're going to put our wrists together like this." And I said, "Oh, no you're not going to cut my wrist off, buster." So we never did that, but that's the way he joked around. Some nights, I was afraid to go to bed just in case he did take that knife out.

He was a great captain. He had a way of motivating us by taking all the blame on his shoulders. A lot of times when we were going bad, he'd come in the room and speak first. "Look, I'm not playing well," he'd say. "And I've got to work harder in practice. I want you guys to push me. You defensemen, if I'm not backchecking, you let me know." "We certainly will let you know, Chief," they'd tell him. He was a guy who would do anything for you. He'd throw a party for us after every season. He was perfect for the role, a natural leader.

Being a captain, you've got a big load to carry. They have to know everything that's going on within the room and within the team. When the coach wants to know, "How come this guy's not playing well? George, you've got to find out why he's not playing well." It was left up to Chief to discover the answer. He would talk to us first because we would listen to George sometimes more than we'd listen to the coach. He was just that way. When he had to talk to someone on the team, he wouldn't say anything, even to me hardly. Sometimes, I'd think, "Chief, where you going?" He'd say, "I'm just going to go downstairs and talk to a couple of the guys." "You want me to come with you?" "No, I don't want you to come with me," he'd snap at me. "You stay here and watch TV or something." When Chief talked, they would listen. He was captain and he'd been in the league a long time. Naturally, you could get some good information from him.

George was a good two-way hockey player. He was a bit of a clumsy skater, but he still did the job. He'd get his share of goals, he got close to 300. Chief was a good person off the

ice and a good hockey player on the ice. Chief scored a lot of
big goals for us. He collected nine goals and 10 assists in 33
Stanley Cup final games, including a pair of game winners.
He assisted on Dick Duff's Cup-winning goal in 1962
against Chicago and also figured in Billy Harris' goal that
kept us alive in Game 6 of the 1964 final against Detroit. We
won that in overtime on Bobby Baun's goal and then took
the Cup by beating the Wings in Game 7. People remember
to this day that it was Chief's empty-netter that iced
Toronto's last Cup win against Montreal in 1967.

He was well-liked by everybody and his attitude towards
others was great, he liked them too! That's probably why he
was with the Leafs for so long, because he was such a solid
team man and captain. There was a lot of harmony in the
room and it was mainly because of George.

We had some real pranksters on those Leafs teams.
Ronnie Stewart was good for a few jokes in the room and so
was Eddie Shack. Shackie was as loose as a goose. He had a
lot of fun at our expense. He'd loosen the guys up.

Still, the king of the practical joke was the Chief. He was
the comedian in the dressing room and more often than not, I
was the butt of his pranks. One time, he hid my false teeth in
the dressing room. I had them in a little box that I kept on the
shelf in my locker. Apparently, the Chief's little bit of
skullduggery took place while I was still out at practice. A
lot of the players had gone off the ice, but I wanted to stay
out because I needed more work, but only one guy would
stay on the ice and that was Larry Hillman. We stayed out
for awhile and when we got into the dressing room, the first
thing I did was reach for my teeth. I took them out and tried
to put them in my mouth and they weren't even my teeth. So
I blamed Eddie Shack at first, because he was a real
prankster, but he said, "Don't blame me this time Johnny.
Blame your roomie." So I asked George Armstrong and he
started laughing, so I knew right off the bat it was him. I
said, "Who are you laughing at? I want to know where did
you get these teeth from?" "Well, you know," he said, "I've

got a buddy who works in a funeral home, so guess who I got them from?"

On the road, I used to go to a grocery store and buy about half a dozen oranges, because I didn't eat breakfast, just a coffee and an orange in the morning. I don't know why, but I was never a breakfast eater. The odd time, if I fancied it, I'd eat breakfast, but not very often. I just couldn't digest my food. I just wasn't hungry. I had to keep my weight down, that was one big reason and I knew there was going to be a big dinner for me around 2 or 3 o'clock. I'd have a steak, a baked potato and a salad. Then I have a little nap for about an hour, an hour and a half. Then Nancy would wake me up and say, "Okay it's time to get ready for the game." I got up, took a shower and was all set to go.

Away from home, though, we'd be on our own for food. So I'd put my oranges in a paper bag and I left them in a drawer. He would take them out while I was sleeping and then he'd put them on the window sill. In the morning when I got up, gee whiz, they were frozen like rocks.

I'd say, "You know George, it's no good when you thaw an orange out." He said, "Yes it is, it's frozen orange juice, just like the stuff you get from Florida." You couldn't even peel them, my breakfast was ruined. But that was just George. He'd play tricks on anybody. Anything he could get a hold of. He cut my necktie a couple of times. He'd put wintergreen on your jockstrap, that would sure make you jump. He did a lot of stupid things, but they were all in fun.

I love the western movies. One time, we were in Boston and I'd just turned the TV on and there was a good western on the tube. It was the Indians against the Red Coats. Well, the Indians are getting beaten really badly. They're getting killed all over the place, they're being shot by the Red Coats. All of a sudden, George gets up off the bed and turns the TV off. I said, "What did you do that for?" "Because I don't want to see that. The Indians must be the worst people in the world. Look at the way they go right into the line of fire and just get picked off. Come on, we're not that stupid." I said, "Okay then, if you want to turn it off, turn it off." "It's always the white man who wins," he used to complain. "It's never the Indians. Always the white man." Well, he gets up off the bed again about 15 minutes later, turns the TV back on and now the Indians are really giving it to the Red Coats. Now I get up, ready to shut it off and he says, "Don't you shut that TV off. Get back on the bed."

After practice sometimes, we'd do a breakaway competition, with milkshakes as prizes. Well, I got to be pretty good at stopping the guys in those one-on-one situations, so the Chief figured he had to help the shooters out. He'd sneak off into a corner when I wasn't looking and then just as the guy was about to shoot, he'd slide a second puck across my field of vision to distract me.

Every once in a while, I'd get him, though. We were playing Montreal in the Stanley Cup finals and George shot the puck right through the net—I don't know how that happened, because he couldn't break a paper bag with his shot. How it ever went through the net, I have no idea. There must have been a little bit of a spot there that wasn't sewn up properly by the officials, or they missed it. So after that, we nicknamed him George "Bullet" Armstrong.

Our families became great friends, too. We used to have parties and the girls would get together when we were on the road for a week or 10 days. Nancy and I get along very well with George's wife Betty and their daughter Betty Anne. They're a very nice family.

On my birthday one year, I got this wonderful picture sketched by Betty Anne. In it, George is dressed up like an Indian. He's in his Leafs uniform, but he's got the headdress on and a bow and arrow and there I am in goal. I'm wearing my pads and I'm in front of the net. He's shooting these arrows at me and I've got a couple stuck in my knee pads already, one in the shoulder and another in the other shoulder and I'm saying, "I don't think this is how other teams warm up their goalies." In the photo, he's drawing another arrow back in the bow, so I said to him, "George, where's this arrow going?" "It's going right for your throat." he said,

"You wouldn't have got me anyway," I told him, "because I would have ducked."

I retired from the Leafs after the 1969-70 season and Chief retired following the 1970-71 season. We both ended up working with the organization. I was a scout and a goaltender coach. At first, George coached the junior Toronto Marlboros, winning Memorial Cups in 1973 and 1975. He even coached Gordie Howe's sons, Mark and Marty, on that 1973 team. Later, he coached the Leafs during the 1988-89 season and like me, also spent several years scouting players. Our desks were side-by-side in the offices at Maple Leaf Gardens.

There were a lot of times when we'd go to junior games and scout together. Most of the times, we'd sit beside each other, but every so often, he'd go sit behind the goal. I don't know why he liked to sit there, because most scouts like to sit high up in the corners. I think maybe he'd go up there and have a little nap, because in the second and third periods, he'd come up and sit with the rest of us. When we'd sit beside each other, there was always a couple of empty seats between us, because he'd always accuse me of looking at his reports. I wasn't looking at his, he was trying to look at mine to find out what I was putting down as far as rating the goaltenders was concerned.

A lot of times, the draft meetings we had were really something. Chief would speak up with his opinion about a player and then I would speak up. There was one time where they got a hold of my form on this forward, who was a right winger like George was, but he wasn't the greatest skater. He was a little bit of a choppy skater, like George was. Chief wasn't a great skater, but he had enough power to get up the ice and back.

Anyway, I rated this guy a five as a skater, just average. I had to rate him the way he played. I saw him about five times and saw the same thing over and over again. Finally, Chief got his say and we compared notes and he wanted to know, "What game were you looking at, Bower?"

"What game was I looking at?" I said.

"The same game as you."

"This guy can really skate," Chief said. "He's a lot better than that."

"A lot better than you, sure, I know that," I told him, "but he's not any better than that." So we kept jawing back and forth and finally he says, "John, as far as I'm concerned, your ratings are way off the mark." "Is that right? Chief, I saw this guy play five times. How many times did you see him?" He says, "Only once." It ended up we didn't draft the guy.

That's the Chief. That's how he operates. He always leaves you laughing. But beyond that, he's a true friend. He'll always be there for you. It's what made him such a great captain and it's why we've got along so well for all of these years.

CHAPTER SIX

THE GLORY YEARS

Once a team like Detroit beats you out of the playoffs, like the Red Wings did to us in the 1961 semi-finals, you play a lot harder for some reason. That's exactly the way the Leafs felt as a team when we arrived for training camp in the fall of 1961. We knew it was time for us to win the Stanley Cup and everybody got on a roll. We had a good team. Punch molded the team together really well with assistant coach and general manager, King Clancy.

A big thrill for me came October 7, 1961, when I played in the NHL All-Star Game at Chicago Stadium. We beat the defending Stanley Cup Champion Chicago Black Hawks 3-1. I played the first half the game, allowing a goal by Eric Nesterenko, then gave way to my old New York Rangers buddy Gump Worsley.

We set an early tone, breaking from the gate 7-2-1 in our first 10 games and we let everyone in the league know we were for real when we went into the Montreal Forum and beat the Canadiens 3-2 to hand them their first defeat of the season. A week later, the Leafs publicity department celebrated my 37th birthday by issuing a release noting that I was the oldest player in the NHL. Always with the age thing.

We were right on Montreal's heels for first place and we actually moved into first place for a brief time in January, a spot where the Leafs hadn't ended a season since the 1947-48 season. The Canadiens pulled away in the second half, finishing 13 points ahead of us and the 85 points we garnered was five short of the club record we'd set in 1960-61.

Still, there was a confident feeling heading into the playoffs and I think it stemmed from the depth and balance of those Leafs clubs. We always stressed defense first. We'd work at our defense a lot. The big thing was in those days if you scored 20 goals, you'd had a pretty good season. Punch would always say, "I would rather have five players on my hockey team score 20 goals and one player like Frank Mahovlich get 38." This way, he could match lines and on every line there was always one or two guys who could score 20 goals and he felt that made our chances better to win the Stanley Cup.

My teammates, wanted to win as much as I did and we'd face our first test against the Rangers, who'd made the playoffs for the first time since 1957-58. It was a tough series. We split the first four games, with the home team winning each time. Game 5 was at Maple Leaf Gardens and was deadlocked after regulation time.

The Gumper played a sensational game that night, making 53 saves. He was so spectacular, even our fans had to applaud his efforts. We both were hot. It was nip and tuck all the way. We went through the first overtime scoreless. Finally, 4:23 into the second overtime period, Red Kelly poked a rebound behind Gumper and we had the win. Afterwards, I led several of our players, including George Armstrong, our captain, down the ice to shake the Gumper's hand. His performance was that impressive.

The victory seemed to spark us, because we whipped the Rangers 7-1 to take the series. Two nights later, we started the finals against Chicago, which had upset Montreal in the other semi-final and we beat the Hawks by 4-1 and 3-2 counts to take a 2-0 advantage, the first time we'd ever had a lead in a Stanley Cup final series.

It didn't last long. Chicago won 3-0 and 4-1 back on home ice and disaster struck for me in Game 4. I pulled my groin doing the splits on a Bobby Hull shot in the first period with the game still scoreless. The guys on the bench knew something was wrong with me. George Armstrong came up to me and said, "Punch says you're not doing too well with your lateral movement and you're not moving around too fast." I said. "I'm okay." He said, "No you're not. John, this is a big game. You can't play hurt." I said, "I'm okay, really I am." I didn't want to put Don Simmons on the spot. "You go tell Punch I said I'm okay." George delayed the game again and came back to me. "Punch told me to tell you that if you don't come out, he's going to fine you $500." Well I think I broke the world's record going to the bench.

Facing Bobby Hull, let me tell you, it was scary, no doubt about that. But when he came down that wing, I wasn't afraid to crouch against him, because I knew he'd either score or I'd get lucky and stop it. He had about the hardest shot in the National Hockey League as far as I'm concerned. He could fire that puck. His brother Dennis actually had a harder shot, but he didn't know where it was going and I didn't know where it was going. Dennis had a high rising shot, whereas Bobby was more accurate. When Bobby shot that puck, you couldn't even see it. It was impossible to stop. And if I did, especially from close in, everybody thought I'd made a great save. But it wasn't that I made a great save, it was more like it hit me. I couldn't see the thing. When he would wind up with that warped stick of his, look out. He had such good control of that stick and there was no whip in it. It was as hard as a rock. Just like a stiff golf club.

I was out for the series and it was up to Donnie Simmons, my back-up, to carry the load. A lot of goalies, me included, find it difficult to come in cold like that, but

Simmons, he didn't mind being a second goaltender. It was tough for a goaltender to do that, to go in after sitting on the bench and have everyone expect miracles from you, but when Donnie's time came to play, he was always prepared to go in. He worked hard in practice to be certain he'd be ready. And he was.

We got into a shootout with Chicago in Game 5, not Punch's style of hockey, but it worked out for us. We beat the Hawks 8-4, with Bobby Pulford firing a hat trick. Game 6 was back at Chicago Stadium and was scoreless until Bobby Hull tallied in the third period. It looked like we were headed back to Toronto for Game 7, but Bob Nevin tied it, then Tim Horton went the length of the ice with the puck and fed a perfect pass to Dickie Duff for the winner. The Stanley Cup was ours.

When we won in 1962, wow, what a great feeling! I was probably the oldest goalkeeper to win his first Stanley Cup. That was a dream come true, a childhood dream to have my name engraved on the Stanley Cup. It was a dream I never ever thought would come true, to be on a Stanley Cup team. I thought, "Boy oh boy, we're going to win a few more" and we sure did. It's a great feeling and a very hard feeling to explain, but a wonderful feeling, for everyone.

That was Toronto's first Cup since 1950-51 and 2,000 people mobbed us at Malton Airport when our flight landed from Chicago. The victory parade that we had was quite the celebration. It started from Maple Leaf Gardens and went right down to City Hall. It was just like when the war ended in 1945. The fans were on the sidewalk trying to get autographs, but there were so many police around they couldn't get near us. The crowd was estimated at 100,000. We were parading down Yonge Street and the tickertape was flying down from the high buildings. After the parade, we went up to mayor Nathan Phillips' office, signed the guest book, heard a little speech from him and got a souvenir pin of the city. It was a great memory and quite the celebration.

We began our defense of the title by handling the NHL All-Stars 4-1. Naturally, the only All-Star to get one by me was the incomparable Gordie Howe. But I'd get even with him in the long run that season.

Once you win one Cup, you want to keep going. But when you win the Stanley Cup, everybody else wants to beat you, because they all want to be champions. When the 1962-63 season started, the other teams were playing a lot harder against us, so you have to play even harder to keep them from getting it.

We were up to the task, because the Leafs were a true team. We were built around defense first and foremost and the defense I had in front of me was outstanding. I had to study my defensemen to know exactly what they were going to do and they studied me, too. A lot of times when I'd fall down and there really was no reason to go down, they'd point out that I could have gotten to the puck quicker by simply using my lateral movement. That's the way it was. We worked together and what a group to work with.

The combination of Allan Stanley and Tim Horton never failed to amaze me. I think they had built-in radar. Allan was fantastic at playing the angle on the shooter and he never obstructed my vision while doing it. He was blessed with tremendous anticipation and seemed to know where I was going to play the rebound even before I did. Nancy and I got along really well with Allan Stanley and his wife Barbara, too.

Timmy Horton, he was such a competitor and he sure was powerful. I remember one night we had a big riot in Boston and he grabbed a hold of a fellow. Punch always said, "Look, when you get into a fight, make sure you push the other guy quite a ways away from you when it's done. If you don't, he'll give you a sucker punch." Anyway, the fight started and Timmy couldn't fight or use his dukes, but he'd get a hold of you in that bear hug and you'd be sorry. He started squeezing this guy really tight. It was right in front of the bench and I could see from looking at him that this guy was starting to turn purple. Timmy finally looked into the guy's eyes, realized it and said, "Have you had enough?" The guy couldn't even answer him, just nod his head a little.

I thought the guy was going to collapse. Timmy let him go, but he forgot to push him and the guy gave him a sucker punch. He got him a good one, right in the eye and his eye was a little black and blue after that.

Of course, he's known today for the donut shops that bear his name, but back then, he was just starting the business. One time, Timmy had just opened another one of his donut shops and he asked a couple of the guys to come down and sign autographs for him and we'd get $25. There was myself, Allan Stanley and George Armstrong. I asked him, "You sure we're all getting $25?" and he said, "Yep, everybody's getting the same money." We get down there and we're signing autographs for two hours. Now it comes time to pay everybody off. He gives $25 each to Allan and George, then he comes to me and says, "I have no money left." I said, "What are you talking about? That cash register is full." He says, "I can't take any money out of that. Look John, we've got a practice tomorrow. I'll pay you off when I get to the dressing room." So I said, "okay" and never thought anything about it again. When I get to practice the next day, I come through the door and turn around the corner of the entrance to where my seat was and I look and there's 18 boxes of donuts. He paid me off in 18 dozen donuts. Can you imagine that? I got them out of there in a hurry before the other players showed up. They were just starting to come in and I got them out of there in time and gave them to the workmen. If Punch would have ever caught me with 18 dozen donuts I would have been riding the buses in the minors for sure.

Our other regular defensive pairing in those days was Bobby Baun and Carl Brewer. Bobby Baun, even to this day, I get along great with him. I see him all the time and he's put on a little weight like all of us, but he's the same person. As a hockey player, he gave it 150 per cent effort every time he was out there. He blocked shots for me, he didn't care who it was. He had a job to do and he was going to do it. He was a good, honest defenseman. He'd go out and he'd hit the guy as clean as he possibly could. If he had to fight, he would, but he didn't look for it. He'd get a few goals, but not that many. He had a good, but wild shot. I don't think he could see the net, to be honest with you. Boomer they called him, because you could hear a big sound around Maple Leaf Gardens every time one of his shots hit the boards. Bobby was a great competitor. There's another fellow the Leafs got rid of too soon that I felt they should have kept.

Carl Brewer was a brainy player. He sure could skate and handle that puck. Carl had it out with Punch several times. Carl was a very nervous defenseman, a good skater and a good playmaker, but he wasn't Punch's style. Punch wanted him to get the puck out of his own end quickly, but Carl liked to go up and skate with the puck and get some good shots on the net. Punch couldn't get him to change and they didn't hit it off too well and Carl left in 1965. Eventually, I guess they did patch things up, though, because Carl came back and played with the Leafs for a while in 1979-80.

We'd picked up Al Arbour from Chicago prior to the 1961-62 season and Al was one of my best shot blockers. He'd save me 15-16 goals a season because he knew how to block a shot. His timing in going down was fantastic. I'd stay up on him. That's one of the big reasons why I learned to stand up more because I knew he was going to go down in front of me and cover the lower part of the net.

Kent Douglas was a rookie with us in 1962-63, in fact he won the rookie of the year award that season, the first defenseman ever to win the Calder Trophy. He had a heavy hockey stick, about a 38 or 39 ounce stick, which is heavy for a defenseman. He used it like a tomahawk. That's why he was such a good guy from the point, because he could fire that puck. He was one of my better defensemen and he was a tough guy, too. Nobody fooled around with Kent Douglas. He'd sit in front of that net and he'd knock you down. He was a competitor. He hated to lose. Many times, when I let in a bad goal, he used to come up to me, tap me on the pads and say, "Don't worry, I'll get it back for you from the point with this big stick of mine." He made me feel good that way. And occasionally, he did get the odd one like that.

We had such balance in attack that season, too, just the way Punch preferred it to be. Frank Mahovlich scored 36 goals, Dave Keon netted 28 and Red Kelly notched 20, with George Armstrong and Bob Pulford each scoring 19 times. Beyond them, Dick Duff, Eddie Shack and Ron Stewart chipped in with 16 apiece.

Pully was a guy who hated to lose. He'd sit on the bench there in the dressing room before the game and he'd be very quiet. You didn't say anything to Pully before the game, so you didn't know what he was thinking about, but whatever it was, it was right, because he was doing everything right on the ice. He was great on the faceoffs, scored us some big goals over the years and was just a good two-way hockey player.

Ronnie Stewart was one of the fastest skaters in the league, when he wanted to go. One time, we were playing in the playoffs against Chicago and his job was to watch Bobby Hull. He followed Bobby Hull wherever he'd go and I think that night, Bobby only got about two shots on goal, when Bobby would usually average about maybe nine shots. Other times, though, Stewie was lackadaisical. He could skate, but he'd go when he wanted to go. George Armstrong would say, "Boy that Ron Stewart could be one of the best skaters if only he wanted to push himself."

One day at practice, Stewie went in goal. I think I was hurt and he put the pads on. I was surprised when he came out. He said he'd played goal as a kid. I was watching him and he looked like he was going to take my job for awhile. I was getting scared. He was catching pucks and having a ball.

Stewie used a small stick, almost like a junior stick it was so short. One day Punch came up to him and he was mad because he was missing a lot of long passes. "Your stick is too short," Punch said. "You've got to go to the same length as the other forwards use." It was at practice, so Stewie went into the dressing room and he got another stick, cut it in half and taped it to the stick he was using and came back on the ice. "He said, "Punch, is this stick long enough?" Well, you should have heard the players. Fortunately, Punch took it as a joke. "But seriously," he said to Ronnie, "You should use a longer stick." "But I can handle it better with a smaller stick." Stewie told Punch. That was Stewie. He did his own thing.

Then there was Shack. He was really something, but I don't care what anybody says, he was a big factor in our team winning Stanley Cups. On game night, he'd be the first guy to urge us on. He'd get in that room about a minute before Punch would come in and he'd say, "Come on guys, we've got to work hard and get these guys." He woke us all up, then Punch would come in and give us his pep talk. He took care of the toughest guys there were. Everybody wanted to fight Shack, because if they could beat Shack, they felt they could tame us. John Ferguson could tell you a lot about that. Punch used to send Eddie out after him all the time. Punch used to keep Eddie Shack on the bench when we were playing Montreal in the playoffs until he could see that Ferguson was doing really well. Ferguson was an aggressive player and his job was to go and screen the goaltender, bother the goaltender and put him off balance. Punch would say, "Okay Eddie, get out there. You know what you have to do." Eddie would go out there and as soon as they put Fergie out, Shack was coming and they both knew it. "I'll take care of their tough guy," that's what Eddie would tell us. Within a matter of a few minutes, Fergie would come at him. When you put Fergie on the penalty bench, it sort of slowed the Montreal club down. Montreal was a good skating club, but they didn't have too many rough guys. It's not that they didn't like the rough going, but they just weren't deep in tough guys. Shackie did a great job for us in that role. Even to this day, he's okay. He does a lot of work for charity. Everybody liked Shackie.

Punch would give players so much leeway, then he would sit them on the end of the bench. Many times he had to do it with Shack, because Eddie wouldn't behave himself. One night, Shack wasn't playing at all. He's on the bench, two periods are gone and there were only a few minutes left in the third and we're losing 2-1. Shack gets up on the bench and the crowd starts chanting, "We want Shack, we want Shack." With about two minutes to go, Punch goes up to Eddie and he says, "You might as well go up and sit with those fans who are yelling for you, because you're not going to get on the ice." Shack said, "Okay, thanks. I might as well go have my shower." He didn't go up and sit with the fans, but he went off to the dressing room. I don't even know why Shack needed a shower that night. He didn't get any sweat on him.

Billy Harris only scored eight goals for us that season, but it would be wrong to underestimate his contribution to the team. He was a good penalty killer. When somebody got hurt, Billy was a big asset to our hockey club. Maybe he didn't get much ice time some nights, but he was always right there when we needed him. Billy was a very quiet player in the dressing room, but a wonderful person. He loved to take pictures of everybody. Hundreds of pictures. Personality-wise, he was just a guy who was liked by everybody.

We battled Chicago for first place right down to the wire. We beat Detroit 6-3 on March 9 to move into a tie atop the standings with the Black Hawks. We downed Chicago 3-0 on March 16, launching a three-game losing skid for the Hawks. When we tied Montreal 3-3 on March 20, we clinched first place, the first Leafs team to come out on top in 15 seasons. It was the tightest race the NHL had seen in years. We finished with 82 points, one ahead of Chicago, three in front of Montreal and only five better than fourth-place Detroit.

We opened the playoffs against the Canadiens and quickly raced out to a 3-0 series lead. We won 3-1 and 3-2 on home ice, then posted a 2-0 decision at the Montreal Forum, the first Stanley Cup shutout of my career. Montreal outshot us 37-23 and stayed alive by taking a 3-1 decision in Game 4, but we closed the Habs out back in Toronto. I had another shutout in a 5-0 verdict.

Detroit upset Chicago in a six-game series and would meet us for the Cup, the first Detroit-Toronto final series since 1949. That meant me and my Saskatchewan fishing buddy, Gordie Howe, were going to face off for Lord Stanley's mug.

Gordie gave me a lot of problems. One year in the playoffs when we played Detroit, he only scored one goal on me, but that was rare. He gave me fits and in fact, scored 49 of his 1071 career goals on me during our NHL careers and another 11 in Stanley Cup play.

There's no doubt that he's Mr. Hockey, the best player in history. I'd put his shot and Bernie Geoffrion's shot down as the hardest to get a read on, but I'd have to put Gordie down as the most dangerous opponent I ever faced. Gordie was great. He could switch hands and shoot just as hard left-handed as he could right-handed. Howe had the strongest, fastest wrists in hockey. A goalie never knew if he'd shoot straight or try for the angle. He would change direction when you were positive he couldn't. The Rocket couldn't equal him in that department.

Gordie was a big guy, a strong guy and so tough in the corners, but he wasn't too bad on me. I was afraid to leave the net against some guys, but if the puck was shot in our own end and I saw Gordie coming, I knew he wouldn't bother me too much, because we knew each other so well. He'd just say, "Look out I'm behind you" so he gave me a warning. Now if it was Ted Lindsay, mind you, things would be different. He's the one that if the puck was shot in, he'd come barreling in there and I wouldn't leave my net. The defensemen on my team would get mad at me, but Lindsay was always clobbering guys. He didn't care who it was. The thing is, since we retired, I've met Lindsay quite a few times in Florida and I wouldn't want to meet a nicer guy in my life. We've had supper together, Nancy, myself, Ted and his wife Joanne. He's not too bad after all.

We set the tone for the finals quickly when Dickie Duff scored twice in the first 68 seconds of Game 1, a 4-2 victory for us. Howe scored twice on me in Game 2, but we won 4-2 again. Detroit gained a 3-2 decision in Game 3, but we weren't going to be denied. Game 4 at the Olympia was ours, again by a 4-2 count. We were going home with a chance to take the Cup and that didn't sit too well with the Detroit fans.

As we left the ice, they pelted us with water bombs, paper clips and foul language. Carl Brewer caught a water bomb right between the eyes. They were mad, but Detroit fans weren't really like that normally. There were those guys who used to throw the octopus on the ice, but beyond them, Detroit fans generally didn't throw stuff. But Punch had the last word before we reached the safety of our dressing room. "Go on home," he told the Detroit fans. "You've seen your last hockey game here this season."

Punch was right. We closed out Detroit at home, winning 3-1, but it went right down to the final bell before Dave Keon hit the empty net with the clinching goal with only five seconds to play. He scored twice in the game, but it was Shack who netted the winner. Like I said, you can call him the clown prince of hockey all you want, Shackie was a big part of our Cup victories.

We beat them in five games and won the Cup in just 10 games, an amazing feat considering that Frank Mahovlich, our leading goal scorer during the regular season, didn't score once in the playoffs. That's what made us so successful, though. Those Maple Leaf clubs had such talented individuals, but we were cohesive and we worked together. I liked being a team man. It was a good, warm relationship and we all needed one another.

After we shook hands with the Wings, Gordie Howe and I stood arm in arm on the ice and did a TV interview with Hockey Night In Canada's Frank Selke Jr. I'd only allowed 16 goals in 10 playoff games, with two shutouts and I felt pretty good about that. In the dressing room, I shared a celebratory drink with my son John. My glass was filled with champagne, his with ginger ale.

A lot of hockey people thought that 1962-63 club was a good team, maybe the best Maple Leafs team ever and certainly the best of the four I won Stanley Cups with. But I always thought the 1961-62 club was a better team than the 1962-63 team. I still maintain that the first Stanley Cup win in 1962 and the one we won in 1967 when everybody said we didn't have a chance because of all the old guys we had, those were the most memorable for me.

Not many people gave us a chance to win in 1963-64, either, but we'd prove the critics wrong that season, too. We started out by drawing 3-3 with the NHL All-Stars, then whipped Boston 5-1 in our season opener. We were only 6-4 through our first 10 games, though. We were in third place at mid-season, seven points back of first-place Chicago and we hit bottom January 18 at Maple Leaf Gardens, when the last-place Boston Bruins hammered us 11-0. Every time I go anywhere, people ask, "What happened in that game you lost 11-0?" The thing is, I didn't even play that night. It was Donnie Simmons. I was out with a hand injury at the time. They called up Al Millar from Denver of the Western League to replace Donnie after that game, but he couldn't get out of Denver because of a snowstorm. So Donnie went back in the next night in Chicago. He shut the Black Hawks out 2-0 and he was a hero again. So there you go, the story of goaltending. You're a bum one day and a hero the next day.

It was around this time of the season that we first started hearing the rumors that the New York Rangers were going to trade star right-winger Andy Bathgate to the Leafs. The talk never subsided and finally on February 22, 1964, the blockbuster was pulled off. We got Bathgate and forward Don McKenney from the Rangers for five players—Bob Nevin, Dickie Duff, Rod Seiling, Bill Collins and Arnie Brown. There was some sadness in the dressing room, sure. You didn't like to see anybody go, but when we got Bathgate, we got ourselves a great goal scorer. That was quite a trade. We were only three games above .500 when the deal was made. After the trade, we lost only four games the rest of the way and Bathgate collected 18 points in 15 games. Punch put Bathgate on a line with Red Kelly and Frank Mahovlich, while McKenney played with Davie Keon and my roomie George Armstrong.

We finished the season in third place with 78 points and would face first-place Montreal in the opening playoff round.

And what a round it was. We split the first two games, then were ahead 2-1 with three minutes to go in Game 3 and blew it 3-2 when J.C. Tremblay scored at 17:25 of the final period and Henri Richard got the winner at 19:35. The emotional blow of that setback could have finished us, but we rallied to take Game 4 by a 5-3 score, with Mahovlich figuring in all five goals. Back in Montreal, the Habs were 4-2 winners in Game 5 and we came home facing elimination. On the off day before Game 6, Punch showed us footage of our series-clinching 5-0 win over Montreal from the previous spring. That night when I got home, I fell ill with the stomach flu and didn't get a lick of sleep. I'd been taking a lot of heat in the press for my play in the series and I wanted to come up big. I did. I stopped 25 shots and we won 3-0, to head back to Montreal for Game 7.

We got a jump with two first-period goals by Keon and it stayed that way until midway through the third period, when the Canadiens got one back. They threw everything they had at me in that frame, but I stopped 17 of 18 shots and Keon put it away with his third goal into an empty net. I finished with 38 saves and was named the game's first star. "We were two goals down, came back and were stopped by Bower," Canadiens managing director Frank Selke told George Gross of the Toronto Telegram. "He's a great goaltender. It eases the pain if you lose to a nice guy like Bower." That was certainly a wonderful compliment to get.

We were going back to the finals and awaiting us was a surprise opponent—fourth-place Detroit, which had upset Chicago, also in a seven-game series.

The final series was remarkably similar to our set with Montreal. It went back and forth. We were even through four games, with three of the first four contests decided by one goal. But Detroit got the edge with a 2-1 win in Game 5 on Eddie Joyal's third-period goal. Things looked bleak for us back at the Olympia when we trailed twice in Game 6. But we went to overtime tied 3-3 and won it when Bobby Baun scored. It was his second goal of the playoffs and just his third and the last he'd ever score in Stanley Cup play, but what made that goal so famous was that Baun scored it while playing with a hairline fracture of the ankle. He'd suffered the injury when hit by a Gordie Howe shot during the third period.

That seemed to take the life out of Detroit and we shut them out 4-0 in Game 7 at Maple Leaf Gardens, becoming the first team ever to win the Stanley Cup by taking consecutive seven-game series. They were do or die situations, but we seemed to be able to pull through those times. I liked pressure. I didn't like standing there doing nothing. I liked it when they kept shooting and shooting. The more they shot at me, the better I got.

Recording a shutout in the Cup-clinching game, I guess I was a little bit excited. I had a habit of throwing my stick into the air when we won big games. We'd just won it and the guys were coming at me pretty fast, because the play was in our end when the game ended. I meant to throw my stick in the corner, but I was so excited, I threw it straight up in the air and all of a sudden, all the players stopped in their tracks. I couldn't understand what was wrong, so I looked up and before I realized it, boom, it hit me on the head. I've still got a scar from the seven stitches. I didn't even feel it, I was so excited. I kept holding my hand to my self inflicted wound, pinching it, to squeeze it together and stop the bleeding. I was happy. I don't know why I did it. Most guys drop their stick or bang it on the ice when they're happy. I'd thrown mine up in the air and then forgot that I'd thrown it.

After the game, Gordie Howe came up to me. He wanted my goal stick. I didn't want his stick after all the trouble he gave me in the series, but we exchanged sticks after the series. He said, "What do you want my stick for?" and I told him, "I want to break it." I really wanted to do that. In the end, I don't think I broke that stick, but I sure wanted to do it.

The only disappointment from those Cup wins was that we only got one Stanley Cup ring. We were supposed to get four rings and we only got one. Something happened, I think somebody pawned a ring or something, so they called us back in and Harold Ballard, who was executive vice-president of the Leafs at the time, he told us they were taking the rings back to have a larger diamond put in them. When we got it back, I said, "It looks smaller than the other one" and George Armstrong said, "You go ahead and tell Mr. Ballard that." Getting only one ring, we didn't think that was a good move by any means, because if you have any children, each one can get one. You take Montreal for example. Henri Richard had 11 and Jean Beliveau had 10 rings. But what are you going to do?

Another thing about that 1964 triumph—Andy Bathgate scored the Cup winner for us against Detroit and Don McKenney, he also had a big playoff for us. It's hard to predict whether we would have won it without that trade, but Punch and the scouting staff must have seen something missing and they made the right move. Punch usually did.

CHAPTER SEVEN

LIFE WITH PUNCH

People don't know this, but I almost quit the Leafs
before I'd ever won the Stanley Cup. It was in 1961. We'd
lost a game and our coach-GM Punch Imlach hated to lose.
On top of that, we didn't play well and we lost by a big score
on the road. We came back to Toronto and when Punch said,
"Ten o'clock on the ice for practice," you'd better be on the
ice for 10 o'clock. We're all sitting on the bench at about one
minute to 10 and we see Punch coming around the corner.
They'd had wrestling at Maple Leaf Gardens the night before
and they hadn't finished sweeping up, so there were a lot of
cigarette butts on the floor around the bench. Eddie Shack
spotted an unused cigarette on the floor by the bench and
asked me to slip it in my glove and save it for him for later.
Then when Punch comes out, Shack says, "Punch, Bower's
smoking a cigarette." Punch asks, "You smoking, Bower?"
and I said kind of sarcastically, "Yeah, I'm smoking all
right," not thinking that Punch probably still wasn't in a

good mood from the night before. So Punch snaps at me, "Get in that room, Bower." We were just joking around, but he was still mad about the game. He looked at me and scowled and demanded, "You want to run the hockey club? I'm the coach and the manager." And I said, "Punch, I didn't want to get Shack in trouble. There's butts from cigarettes all over. I dropped my glove and when I picked it up, I saw a cigarette butt drop out of my glove. That's all there was, there was no lighting up." But we had a pretty good set-to and after it was over with, I said, "Punch, I'm leaving. I'm quitting. I can't take this pressure from you anymore. I'm going home." So I told George Armstrong, our captain, that I was quitting. He said, "You can't do that to the players. You're a key man." I said, "I'm not quitting on them, I'm quitting on Punch." He said, "Punch is your boss. You've got to do what you're told to do." So he called me back later in the day and he told me, "Look, you'd better come back to practice at 10 o'clock in the morning." So I came back the next day and Punch looked at me. "Well, I'm glad you made practice" and he sort of grinned in a way that meant we were back being friends again.

There was another time that Punch and I really had it out and it was in 1964 over an incident involving Montreal Canadiens tough guy John Ferguson. Boy, Punch sure got mad at me that time. The game before in Montreal, Ferguson ran right into me and you know he hurt me, put me out of commission for a little while. He just about knocked me out. When I got my breath back, I told Ferguson, "Fergie, I'm going to get you. When I don't know, but if you ever come through my goal crease again, I'll give you my goal stick." So this particular time, we're playing in Toronto, beating Montreal 6-1 and I saw my opportunity. I saw him coming down the wing and Fergie never cut in front of the goaltender. He'd go right for you, it didn't matter whether or not the puck was around. This time, he came at me and I gave him the poke check. I missed the puck, but I got my stick right between his legs and he went flying hard right into the corner. I left the net and I said to him, "Are you okay?"

He looked up and said, "Yeah, I'm okay. And you better keep your head up."

Well, Punch had seen me do this and when I got to the dressing room, Punch said to me, "You know, I don't understand you, Bower. The guy just about killed you that night and you get him back and then you go out of your net to see him? What did you say to him?" I said, "I just wanted to know if he's okay." Now, Punch is getting mad. "I don't want any prima donnas on this hockey club. This isn't kindergarten. We're playing to win here. You do that again and you'll be riding the buses." Punch was so mad, he sat me out for a week, but he told the press that I had injured my hand. He didn't want there to be any controversy about the decision.

Punch was like that. He would never knock his players in public. A couple of times after the first period of games, I went to Punch and I said, "Look, I'm hurting the team, I'm not playing the way I should. I let in a bad goal and I don't know what I was thinking. I can tell myself I'm not me. He was understanding and he'd put Terry Sawchuk or Bruce Gamble in. But when the press would ask Punch why he took Bower out, he'd say, "Well, he wasn't feeling well." He'd never give them the right information as to why he pulled me out of the game.

Punch was that kind of a person. He could get into you and get you mad and he didn't care if you got mad at him. He just wanted to know what worked with you, what made you tick. He sized everybody up. He knew how he could talk to me and how he could talk to Frank Mahovlich. When Frank was traded in 1968, I was ready to quit. And I wasn't afraid to tell Punch what I thought when he traded Frank to Detroit. "You traded my best player," I told him. "Your best player?" he yelled. "That's right," I told him. "You traded my best left winger. He's our best goal scorer." He said, "You just play goal and don't worry about anybody else." He shut me up there pretty good again.

Other times, he could be really understanding. He would tell us, "Okay, we got clobbered, but it was just one game, so let's forget about it. We're going to work on our mistakes, watch some film, see what we did wrong." He was good that way. A lot of players figured he wasn't a good coach, but a better manager, but he was both as far as I was concerned. Everybody had their own opinion.

Punch would talk to anybody who wanted to talk. He brought players in and they had their own talk about things. If you weren't playing well, he wanted to know why you weren't playing well. If there were any problems you wanted to discuss, he would listen. That's part of management's job.

For the most part, my relationship with Punch was just great. I remember Punch when he coached Springfield of the American Hockey League. I was in Cleveland and we had a great series against them. I guess he must have remembered that, because I think he was a big factor in me being drafted by the Toronto Maple Leafs. I had a meeting with him and he said, "Johnny, I don't care if you're a hundred years old, if you can play for me and do your work like you can, we'll be fine. I understand through my sources that you work as hard in practice as you do in the game and that's what I like to see, good solid hard work. I expect that from everybody, not only you. But right now I'm talking to you. I want you to do what you're told to do and work hard in practice for an hour, an hour and a half every day and what you do after that I really don't care. Do your job and you'll produce and eventually you'll improve. If you go through the motions, you're not going to get anywhere. You only get from your game what you put into it." I believed him. That was good advice and he kept his word.

It's not that hard to listen to somebody that's paying you to play a sport that you love. He just wanted things his own way. He was a smart man, a good businessman. He knew figures and he seemed to be a step ahead of everybody. He and his assistant King Clancy would spend hours in the dressing room analyzing film. A lot of guys didn't know that, but they'd spend hours dissecting the films and finding mistakes that the other team was making that we could exploit. Punch was a very dedicated manager and coach.

He expected the same level of dedication from the players and if he felt he wasn't getting it, look out. When we weren't going to his satisfaction, quite often he'd hold two-a-day practices. If we didn't play well, that's the way he was. We'd go on the ice in the morning, then he'd make us come back in the afternoon, because he was there all day anyway. It didn't matter to him. We'd go in the afternoon from 2-4, just when the traffic was starting to build up as you all got ready to go home. And your wife was waiting, she had supper for you. Now he's got the wives mad because your meal is either all curled up and cold or burnt, depending upon what kind of a cook you had at home.

Having King Clancy around as Punch's assistant coach and GM really helped Punch out, too, because they worked almost a good cop, bad cop scenario between the two of them. Clancy was a guy who would always step in there when there was a problem. A lot of guys, when they were having trouble with Punch, they would go to King Clancy and say, "Can you help me out?" Clancy, having been a hockey player himself, would help everybody out. He even told me a lot of times, "John, you're falling down too much. You've got to stand up and challenge the shooter." I'd say, "King, sometimes you've got to go down," and he'd say, "Yeah, but you're going down before you should be going down. You've got to wait until that guy shoots the puck. Then you can make your move. You're going down on your knees before he shoots and then he's got four openings on you." Then he'd pat you on the back and say, "Just practice that. That's all you have to do and it'll come to you." He was a big help to all the players and well liked by everybody. There was only one King Clancy.

Punch was rigid in his rules in terms of how he wanted the game to be played. One day, we were not playing to Punch's liking and he said, "I'm sick and tired of you guys giving the puck away in your own end. From now on, everybody who gives the puck away in our own end is going to be fined five dollars." Well, five dollars was a lot of money in those days. And Punch saw me grinning and he said, "That goes for you too, Bower." From that point on, anytime the puck came into my own end, I would stop it right there and leave it for one of my defensemen. The poor guys had to hustle back to get it. And they're yelling at me, "Shoot it, Shoot it," but if I shot it and the other team intercepted the pass, then I'm the guy who was going to pay the five dollars. I paid a couple of fines, but mostly it was a bad situation whenever I got the puck, because of the arthritis in my hands. I could stop it, but I'd just knock it down and put it in the corner. The defensemen used to get mad at me all the time. These guys all had bonuses for goals for and goals against and they wanted that puck out of our end as soon as possible. But I'll tell you what. When it was all over with, we weren't giving the puck away too much in our own end.

Punch had all kinds or rules like that. Lose a faceoff, it cost you five dollars. Bad pass, another five dollars. But we won four Stanley Cups playing for him, so you could say that it worked out okay.

He also hated it when ex-Leafs would come into Maple Leaf Gardens and have a big game against Toronto. I remember we were playing Boston one night and Ron Stewart got a goal on me on a power play and Punch, he sure got mad. He didn't like anybody he'd traded to get a goal against us.

Punch would frequently come up to me and say, "Hey, I want you to stand up." All the time, he'd be saying, "Stand up. Stand Up" and I'd say, "You know, you have to fall down sometimes." He'd just say, "Stand up." I'd go home and that's all I'd hear all night long in my head was "Stand up. Stand up."

He was demanding of all the players and like I said earlier, some fellows didn't like Punch. He wanted to do things his own way, but he mixed it up with the guys pretty well on the plane. He played cards with Mr. Clancy and sometimes, we'd get in a game with Punch and Clancy, gin rummy or something like that. I got along fine with Punch. I can only speak to the way somebody treated me and he treated me fine. Mind you, I would have liked the paychecks to have been a little higher from him. There was a budget, he always told me, "I've got a budget, I've got a budget" and I'd say, "I've got a budget, too. I've got a wife and three kids." "Well, John, I think you're going to do well here," he'd tell me. "You're going to get a big pension." I said "Good." I'm still waiting for it.

Punch wasn't always bad when it came to negotiating. During the 1967-68 season, he actually gave me a raise. We'd just beaten Montreal 5-0. Punch always liked beating the Canadiens and when he came into the dressing room after the game, he smiled at me and said. "I'll tear up your contract and give you a new one tomorrow—with a raise."

The raise was $100 a week, which amounted to an additional $2,400 over the course of the season. "This is the first time I've ever ripped up anyone's contract, but he deserved it," Punch told George Gross of the Toronto Telegram. "You might accuse me of getting soft, I don't care. I had to give it to him."

Most times, though, it was easier squeezing moisture out of a stone than another dollar out of Punch. In 1969-70, the last year I played for the Toronto Maple Leafs I earned $25,000. That's the best I ever got. Punch would line your contract with bonuses for winning things like the Vezina Trophy, then if you had a chance to get it, he'd call up a couple of minor-league defensemen late in the season, just to make sure you'd give up a few goals. Why he did that, I don't know.

He also gave me a raise in 1966-67, but it was quite a battle and it was started by George Armstrong. George asked me at that particular time, "How much money are you getting?" and it was $11,000. "Eleven thousand?" he said. "You've got to be up with the rest of the guys making at least between $15,000 and $18,000. You should even come close to $20,000. You're the best goalie we've got. No one can take your job." "George, I said, "I'm 42 years old." "Don't worry," he said, "You'll get it." He shouldn't have been telling me stuff like that, but he was trying to help me out.

Anyway, I said, "Okay, I'll stick to my guns when I negotiate." And I did stick to my guns. And Punch threw me out of his room three separate times. I went in and said, "I want a raise." Punch asked, "What kind of a raise do you want?" I said, "Ten thousand dollars" and he opened the door and told me to get out. I talked to George again and he said, "Don't give in." The next time we met, Punch said, "Johnny, this is your last chance. Either sign or I might have to send you down to the minors." I said, "Can I think about it?" and he said, "Well, don't think about it too long." I went and told George and he said, "He won't send you to the minors. He's got nobody else after Terry Sawchuk except Bruce Gamble. Bruce Gamble is a good goalie, but he can't carry your stick, John." So I came back and told Punch, "I'm, sorry, but I'm not going to sign." He said, "You're not?" and that's when Clancy came walking into the room and said, "What's going on?" So I told him, "My wife's pregnant and everything else—she wasn't pregnant, though, I lied—and I'm trying to get a raise and he won't even give me anything." He said, "How much do you want?" and I said, "I'm, asking for $10,000. I have to be up there with the other veterans." "Ten thousand?" Clancy said. "We can't give you that, we're on a budget. Frank Mahovlich isn't even making that." I thought, "I'm not interested in Frank's or anybody else's contract." So he says, "John, will you take a $5,000 raise?" and of course, Punch near about fell off his chair. "You're not getting $5,000. You're not getting anything," he yelled. I said, "What's that you said King? You'd give me a $5,000 raise?" He said, "Yes," and I said, "Where's the pen?" So I signed it and got the $5,000 raise. Punch just looked at me, scowling and said, "You'd better get on that ice and you'd better have a good year or I'm going to take that $5,000 back from you." But he never did. In fact when we won the Stanley Cup, I got a bonus of $5,000, so I got my $10,000 in the end.

Punch was well-connected in the community and he could get things done for you off the ice, too. One time there, I took our car in. Nancy had a little GM convertible and she said it needed painting. I said, "Look, I'll take it to training camp in Peterborough with me and talk to Punch." We had a great fan there in Peterborough who ran a General Motors dealership, a fellow by the name of Jack McGee. He was a good friend of Punch's and a great hockey fan. You could hear him yelling all over the rink. So I asked Punch, "Do you think you can get me a paint job? You know, a fairly cheap job, because I haven't got much money to spend." He said, "How much money to do you want to spend?" and I said. "Not very much." "So you want a cheap, cheap paint job? "I said, "Not real cheap, but I want to get rid of all the dents." So anyway, one day, later during camp, he comes to me and says, "I want you to leave it with me and I'll take it over to the auto body shop." Just before we were going to break from training camp, we had a golf tournament and everybody had to play. And if you didn't golf, you had to caddy for someone. That's when Punch took the keys and left the car at this dealership in Peterborough. He got the car painted for me. I had a French-Canadian goaltender caddying for me during the golf tournament. He could hardly speak any English at all. Along about the 17th hole, Punch was behind us and he yelled for this kid to come over and see him. When the kid came back he says to me in broken English, "Mr. Imlach told me to tell you that your car was ready at the clubhouse. You can see it from here." So I looked and there was Nancy's car and it was every color of the rainbow—red, black, blue, green. The guys got a real bang out of it. I didn't know what to do with it so George Armstrong says, "Oh quit complaining, I'll drive it back to the hotel for you." So George drove and I scrunched down in the front seat next to him and he's yelling, "Hey, Johnny Bower's in here. It's his car, not mine." That's the kind of comedian he was.

That night we had a curfew, but I took it back to Nancy, because I didn't want to drive it around Peterborough. When

I showed it to Nancy, she said, "Who did that?" and I said, "Punch." "Well, you take it right back and get it done right." So I got back about 2:00 in the morning, but Punch never did catch me, which was a good thing, because I would have been fined $25 for being out after curfew. I found out he was playing a joke on me. It was water colors. Thank God for that. They ended up painting it light blue.

Most of the time, Punch's words about me were very flattering. He said that I had more guts than anyone in professional sports. It was a nice comment for my coach to say, but I don't know that I had more guts than anyone else. I was a goaltender and I wanted to play goal. I couldn't play anywhere else. I worked hard at my position. He liked somebody that worked very hard in practice. That was Punch's key. He felt that about everybody—if you worked, you'll get somewhere. Us older guys had to work. The younger guys, they could slow down a little, but they had the legs. They could work past it. When the game started, we all worked together.

He also liked to tell everyone that I was the greatest athlete in the world. I remember in 1965, there was a big debate as to who would win the honor as Canadian athlete of the year. The debate was between Chicago Black Hawks star Bobby Hull and Olympic runner Bill Crothers, but Punch insisted they had the wrong guys. "I'm taking nothing away from Hull or Crothers," Punch told Jim Coleman of the Toronto Telegram. "They're the boys who have been exciting the public in 1965. But I wonder what Hull and Crothers will be doing athletically when they're 41?" I couldn't believe that. When he was quoted as saying that, well, what a great feeling that was, an honor even. Anything that came out of Punch's mouth, he meant it in a good way, but I couldn't believe he'd say something like that. But it was sure nice to hear. Maybe it was because I believed in working so hard. Try your heart out, work the best that you can and you'll succeed, that was the motto I followed.

Punch was often a stubborn and uncompromising man and a lot of times, he said a lot of bad things in the dressing room, but deep down, Punch meant well. He wanted the team to win and most of all, wanted what was best for the team as a whole.

Eventually, when he did throw a party for us, he threw a great party. He took care of the wives, too. And I saw him do some wonderful things to help out others. If the referees didn't have a flight out after the game, he'd let them ride on the Leafs' charter, which was actually against league rules. He'd hold the plane to allow reporters time to file their stories, even though those stories might have been critical of his team. On one occasion, Duane Rupp's son underwent surgery in Toronto Sick Children's Hospital and Punch called Rupp up from Rochester so that he could be with his son.

Sure, he wasn't perfect, none of us are, but Punch was great as far as I was concerned.

CHAPTER EIGHT

ONE MORE FOR THE AGED

It wasn't long after we'd won our third Stanley Cup in the spring of 1964 when the Leafs claimed goaltender Terry Sawchuk from Detroit in the NHL intra-league draft. It was quite a shock to me, not because I was worried about keeping my job, but because I was really surprised that Detroit would let a goaltender of that caliber go. When we got Sawchuk, I told Punch Imlach right off the bat, "I don't know how you got him, but we're going to win another Stanley Cup." "You think so?" he said. "I know so. This guy's the best goaltender there is in the league." "Well," Punch says, "He's been having some problems, personal problems which I don't have to discuss with you, but I just wanted your opinion." "I'm telling you, we'll win the Stanley Cup with him." And we did. He was sensational. He came in and played sensationally when I got hurt in the 1967 playoffs.

Sawchuk was the one guy that I used to watch in practice that I really couldn't pick up much from. I'd watch him and I liked the way he coasted out on his angles very slowly and with his reflexes, he could move really quickly. Some goalies come out too fast and they lose their balance. He would glide out on a perfect angle and he knew exactly when he had to move sideways to protect his angles. Off the ice, he was very, very quiet. Terry had personal problems, but outside of that, he played well for us.

We actually went to training camp in 1964 with three future Hall of Fame goalies on the roster—Sawchuk, myself and Gerry Cheevers. That was really something. Cheevers was still trying to make the grade. He'd filled in for me for two games during the 1961-62 season, but had spent the rest of his first three seasons as a pro in the minors. I knew that feeling.

I helped Gerry a great deal with the poke check and he gave me a great deal of credit for it. In fact, one year in training camp, he was doing so well with it that I figured I might have to teach him a few bad angles to protect my job. He turned out to be a doggone good pokechecker. In the spring of 1965, Punch left Cheevers unprotected in the draft and he went to Boston. I guess Punch figured he'd maybe keep Terry and I for another year. When he was gone I was really sad to see Gerry go. He was a real competitor and he liked to challenge guys. He'd really come far out of his net. I knew he was going to have a great career in the NHL and he certainly did.

Early during the 1964-65 season, a milestone day arrived in my life. November 8 was my 40th birthday and one of the Toronto papers wanted to make a big deal out of it. They sent a reporter and a photographer out to the house to do a story and Nancy had prepared a beautiful cake for the celebration, but it was in the downstairs fridge and the fridge was locked. I went across the street to the neighbors to get a hammer and a chisel to open the lock. We broke the lock and of course, as soon as we did that, we found the key.

The two-goalie system was an adjustment for me. I guess with me turning 40, Punch was worried about how much game I had left in me, but I thrived on hard work and I wanted to play every game. I felt that at my age, I had to play every game. I wanted to keep playing.

Sawchuk was different. Punch knew Sawchuk could sit on the bench for 40 minutes, then come in and play a sensational game. He didn't need a warmup. That's the way he was in practice, too. He never worked hard, except in the game. Sawchuk could stand there. He didn't need the warmups like I did. He figured he'd save all his good playing for the game, which he did, but in practice, he didn't try as much as I did. You'd shoot the puck in practice and if you hit him, you hit him. If you didn't, it went in. He waved at shots more than anything else. Punch knew he could put Sawchuk in at any time, whereas Bruce Gamble and I, we still weren't the same until we had a good solid warmup.

At one point during the season, Terry had played about eight games in a row and I was getting antsy to get back in there. We were having a shooting drill and I told Eddie Shack in practice, "Look, don't hurt Terry, don't hit him on the throat or anything like that, but if you get a chance to put him out, I'll buy you the biggest steak in Toronto." He looked at me and said, "Yeah?" Shack had a good, heavy shot, you could really feel it when it hit you. Sawchuk was standing there, doing nothing as usual and Shack came in and took a shot. Sawchuk waved at it with his glove hand and it broke his little finger. I just couldn't believe it. I told Shack to do it, but how it ever happened was unbelievable. Sawchuk threw his glove off and went in the dressing room. He'd fractured his finger.

That season, we alternated in the net. In those days, the rule stated that the goalie who played the most games for the team with the fewest goals against got his name on the Vezina Trophy. I'd won it in 1960-61 and Terry, he'd won it three times with Detroit—in 1951-52, 1952-53 and 1954-55. At the start of the season, we shook hands and I said, "Terry, no matter what happens, if I win the grand Vezina myself, I'll split the prize money with you." He said, "Okay, likewise." As it turned out, he played two more games than I did, 36-34 and we won the Vezina Trophy.

It came right down to the wire. On the second-last night of the season, we lost at home 4-1 to Detroit and that put Red Wings goalie Roger Crozier ahead of us, 173 goals against to 175. We would close out the season the next night, March 28, 1965 at Detroit and Punch gave me the start. Terry dressed for the game and sat on the bench, even though it wasn't an NHL rule to suit up two goalies for the game until the following season, but Punch wanted him to be part of it. But Terry went and hid in the dressing room for much of the game. "I was too nervous to watch for two periods," he told me afterwards. I stopped all 37 shots Detroit aimed at me and we won 4-0. The Vezina was ours.

Well, eventually it was ours. Shortly after the season, NHL President Clarence Campbell announced the league was changing the Vezina rules and both Terry and I would get our names inscribed on the trophy. When it was all said and done, Terry kept his word and I kept my word. We threw a big party at the end of the season and it cost us more than the money we earned for winning the Vezina. I think it cost us $500-$600 each, but it was worth it.

We finished fourth that season and would face Montreal in the first round of the playoffs. We held serve through the first five games of the set, with the home team winning every time. Montreal came to Maple Leaf Gardens for Game 6 holding a 3-2 series edge. We carried a 3-1 lead into the third period, but the Canadiens rallied to tie it, then won when Claude Provost scored 16:33 into overtime. Our Stanley Cup reign was over.

In the off season, it was time to go to work. Hockey players didn't make the kind of money in those days that players pull in today, so we all needed to get summer jobs to make ends meet.

I got out of the restaurant and motel business when Nancy and I decided to settle in Toronto year round in the early 1960s and got a job with Borden Chemical, a packaging company in Toronto. It was a good job, very interesting, I enjoyed it. I'd go to a number of different grocery stores and try to sell them packaging film that was used to wrap meat and vegetables. I was what you'd call a troubleshooter. There were a lot of times when other salesman couldn't get an order filled, but I never had any trouble. When they knew I was Johnny Bower, the hockey player, I could get a good-sized order if I promised them a couple of hockey tickets. It cost me a lot of my passes, but it got me a lot of orders. Once in a while, they'd give me some vegetables to take home to my wife.

Punch was wheeling and dealing again in the summer of 1965 and he acquired us another veteran future Hall of Famer in defenseman Marcel Pronovost from Detroit. Marcel was 35 at the time, a veteran of 16 NHL seasons and what a great defensemen he was for me. Why Detroit ever let him go, I'll never know. Maybe because of his age, I don't know, but that's about all I can figure. Was I ever glad to see him. He was a great guy for deflecting shots away from the net and into the corner of the rink. You have to be sharp to do that, to be able to anticipate a pass and stick that stick out into the lane to disrupt it. He really had it upstairs, smart. He would get the odd goal, but he was just a very good defensive player in front of me.

That was Punch's style and I think he was right. Most of the guys he brought in were older fellows and he had a lot of success with them. He knew how they could play and he knew they were competitors, leaders, whatever you want to call it, on the ice and he wanted these older fellows to help the younger fellows develop. A lot of times after practice and in the skating sessions I noticed he'd put an older guy with a younger guy and you see they'd end up talking, maybe about the younger guy's mistakes, maybe about ways the older player could help him with what he was doing wrong. He had a good theory on bringing in the older guys. He felt experience was so important to the team and it would allow the younger players more time to develop in the minor leagues.

In 1965, I was approached by a chap named Chip Young, who worked as a storyteller on the CBC's morning show. He talked to Punch to see if it was okay, then he came into the dressing room and said he'd come up with a song called Honky The Christmas Goose, with Banjo The Mule on the other side of the 45 and he wanted to know if anybody on the team would be interested in singing these songs. I've never seen so many guys undress and get into the shower so quickly in my life. I was the only one left sitting there. He said, "I guess you're the only one left." And I said. "Look sir, I can't sing. Sure, I do my thing in the shower like everybody else." He said, "Won't you try it?" And I pointed toward the showers and said, "There's better singers in there now. Ronnie Stewart likes to hum. Get him." And he said, "Well, there's just something about you that seems right for this. Wouldn't you want to at least try it?" and I relented and said, "Okay." I came home and told Nancy and showed her the music and she said, "Let's sing it together." My son Johnny was downstairs, so we all started singing Honky The Christmas Goose together and she said, "You know, this is cute. It's a nice children's record. If you only knew how to sing." I said, "I know. That's the big problem."

To solve it, first of all, I started to drink tea and honey like all the professional singers said you were supposed to do, because it was easy on your throat. "Don't drink Coke," they told me, "because you'll burp." We practiced it and got to know the words really well. When we got to the studio, my son was involved with it and some other neighborhood kids. Our band was known as Johnny Bower with Little John and the Rinky-Dinks. I'll tell you, those kids were really good singers. When we went to record it, that was the night they had the big blackout all through Toronto and across the Eastern seaboard. I started singing and all of a sudden all of the lights went out. I thought, "Oh John now you've done it." I thought I'd blacked out the whole city just with my voice. We had to wait and wait and I got thirsty, so I went over to the pop machine and got myself a Coke. Well, sure enough, then the lights come back on we started to sing and halfway

Fans are always sending me touching items like this one I received.

A thank you note from a fan after I signed his Leafs sweater.

This fan wrote to me after I posed with her in our basement.

Getting ready to tee it up at a charity golf event with legends Steve Shutt and Don Cherry.

While vacationing in Florida, I had the opportunity to share an elephant ride with my granddaughter Staci.

Another day at the golf course. What could be better!

This young fan was part of a charity golf event at which I appeared.

I love getting out and meeting people. And if I can get in a round of golf at the same time, all the better.

Posing with my foursome prior to a celebrity golf event.

These guys were my playing partners at a charity golf tournament.

Ken Broderick, who played goal in the NHL with Minnesota and Boston, now is a Tim Horton's franchisee. He helped organize this golf event.

A letter I received from a fan in Cleveland.

Two goalies at a Maple Leafs fantasy camp share a moment with an old Maple Leafs goalie.

My old gear in the dressing room stall at Maple Leaf Gardens.

Keeping my eyes on the puck during AHL action with the Cleveland Barons.

Here I am sitting next to my dear friend and the author of my book, Bob Duff while we take a break from working on The China Wall.

I was truly honored when Toronto decided to honor my number along with Walter "Turk" Broda. My family and I cheered as they raised the banners at Maple Leaf Gardens.

In 1967 when Toronto won the Stanley Cup finals, I received two bottles of champagne. One I opened for my 50th wedding anniversary and I saved the other bottle for when the Leafs win the Stanley Cup. As you can see I still haven't had the opportunity to open the Leafs victory bottle (but hopefully I will soon).

Nancy and I meet with Immortal Investments Publisher, Mike Reddy, Author, Bob Duff, and our grandson Johnny III to discuss producing this book.

The Barons wives and children posed for this photo. That's Nancy on the end, the attractive one holding the goalie stick.

A Christmas card we received from minor-league teammate Pete Leswick and his family.

Taking a break from the action during a game with the Cleveland Barons.

Cleveland team photo from 1950–51, the first season that coach Bun Cook opted to go with me exclusively as his No. 1 goalie. We won the Calder Cup title that season.

I learned a lot about playing the game from Bun Cook, my coach in Cleveland. He was a Hall of Famer with the New York Rangers.

We won the AHL Calder Cup title in 1947–48, my third season in Cleveland, but I watched as Roger Bessette handled the goaltending load in the playoffs.

The 1945–46 Cleveland Barons, my first pro team. I'm the one in the goalie pads to the right of the front row.

I was a seasoned pro by 1946–47, my second pro season, splitting goaltending chores with Roger Bessette.

We won another Calder Cup title with Cleveland in 1952–53 and I was named to the AHL's First All-Star Team.

The action gets heated in front of my net during a game with Cleveland.

This is the cover of the "Honky the Christmas Goose" song. At the time it was produced it was the highest selling Canadian produced record. It sold over 40,000 records.

My face was cut for more than 200 stitches during my career.

Shaking hands with Tod Sloan, my teammate in Cleveland during the 1949–50 season.

Two of my Cleveland teammates feel the stress of playoff hockey.

News release from the American Hockey League when I was named MVP.

Players are tumbling all over the place as the action gets heated in this Cleveland game.

Celebrating our 1952–53 AHL Calder Cup win. We took the final series in seven games from Pittsburgh.

Surrounded by several of my old Maple Leafs teammates.

Nancy and I share a night out on the town in Buffalo with Bobby Ochs, one of our trainers in Cleveland and his girlfriend Charlotte Tuttle.

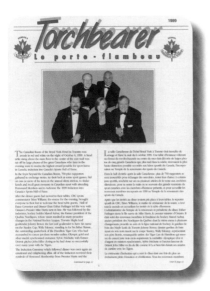

I'm enshrined in nine halls of fame. This is news of my induction into the Canada Sports Hall of Fame in 1999.

Friends and family gathered to celebrate my birthday.

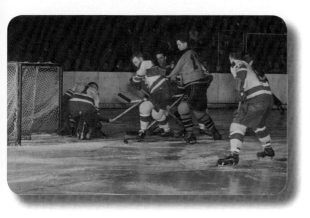

I'm pressed tight against my post, making a save while with Cleveland.

Nancy and I enjoying an evening out with friends Don Daynard, Eric Russell, John Brier, Eleanor McGregor, and Angela Daynard.

We've got plenty to scream about. We've just defeated Pittsburgh to win the AHL Calder Cup title in 1951.

Me and my best girl Nancy.

Nancy and I are enjoying ourselves at this banquet celebrating Cleveland's 1951 Calder Cup triumph.

Joining in conversation with several hockey luminaries, including George Armstrong and Bill Hewitt.

The New York Rangers fan club presented me with this award as the team's most popular player in 1953–54.

Even in a shirt and tie, I'm positioned and ready to stop the shot.

Enjoying the holiday season with the kids in Toronto.

Even as a youngster, it was obvious that my daughter Barbara was destined for skating greatness.

Sharing a laugh with Stan Obodiac, the long-time publicity director for the Toronto Maple Leafs.

That's my birthday cake on the table, in front of banners recognizing the four Stanley Cups I won in Toronto.

Enjoying a cola while talking with Lloyd Saunders, a sportscaster I knew when I lived in Saskatoon.

Fans gather around the goal to snap pictures of me and fellow Toronto goalie Don Simmons.

The kids are excited about their gifts during the Leafs Christmas party.

Nancy gets a ride around the ice from our daughter Cindy during the Leafs Christmas party.

Kicking out my right pad to make a save for the New York Rangers against the Leafs, my future team.

Covering the puck in the goal crease against the Montreal Canadiens, who we played three times in the Stanley Cup final.

The puck is airborne precariously above my head, but I'm focussed and ready to corral it.

Signing autographs sure makes you hungry. Getting something to eat during a charity event in Toronto.

Three of my Toronto teammates— Bob Baun, Tim Horton and Frank Mahovlich—pose for pictures at Maple Leaf Gardens.

Frank Mahovlich and I take a break from signing autographs during a charity function.

A number of Leafs get ready to hit the buffet line, including Dave Keon and Frank Mahovlich.

A young Dave Keon and I are all smiles. Keon followed my good buddy George Armstrong as captain of the Leafs.

Allan Stanley and I were teammates in both New York and Toronto.

Smiling and signing a few photos for some fans.

They still line up to get my signature and it still feels like a honor to me that people care so much.

I don't know how many times I've written my name on pucks, cards, or photos, but I know that it never gets tiring.

"THE KING"
FRANCIS MICHAEL CLANCY

No one gave more to the game of hockey than King Clancy.

Nancy and I together at a charity function.

Nancy and I chatting with one-time NHL defenseman Ivan Irwin, who was my teammate in New York.

I've shared many a moment over the years with my best friend and roommate in Toronto, George (Chief) Armstrong.

I don't remember which one of us told the joke, but both former NHLer Ivan Irwin and I seemed to get a pretty good laugh out of it.

My daughter Cindy and I
alongside the Vezina Trophy,
which I won twice as a Leaf.

The members of the 1967 Cup
champion Maple Leafs were
depicted on this lithograph.

Meeting Leafs fans never gets
tiring, except when they ask me
to explain why we haven't won
the Cup since 1967. Also pictured
Mr. Goalie, Glenn Hall.

Posing with a couple
of Leafs fans.

I love being around children.
This was taken during a benefit
which raised $42,000 for cancer
research.

These two youngsters got to
hold the Stanley Cup in their
Toronto sweaters.

Every year, I go with the NHL Alumni to B.C. to fish for salmon.

When Dunnville, Ontario won the OHA Senior title, they invited me to join the celebration and presented me with a commemorative championship shirt.

Hanging my Maple Leafs flag with pride over the door of our Mississauga home.

Talking things over with a fan while signing some autographs.

These young fellows know who their favorite goaltender is.

through, I burped. "Cut," Chip yelled. "I told you not to have any Coke, but you wouldn't listen." We waited for awhile, then I said my throat was clear now.

We cut it in four or five tries and it turned out really well for us. Musically, that was really a tough year for me. We were bucking the Beatles at the time. They had a pile of records out. In fact, I went to Eaton's across from the Gardens one day. I was sitting there, selling my records and there's a big pile of Beatles records sitting on the table right next to me. So I took their pile of records and put them underneath the table and after that, we were selling all of mine.

The record was a big hit. We made it to No. 29 on the CHUM charts in Toronto and as high as No. 45 on the Toronto Telegram's After Four's Hot 100. The first 7,000 singles sold before the record even hit the stores. We sold about 40,000 of those records, which at the time made Honky the biggest-selling Canadian-made record ever and today, everybody is looking for it. I get asked all the time, "Where can we get this record? We'll pay you well for it." I've got one record at home. It's framed and on the wall and that's the only one I have. "You've got to get it done again," people tell me. I've got a few tapes that I pass along to radio stations. There's one guy in Quebec who plays it every Christmas.

After a bit, Chip Young said, "Boy John, everything went so well, now we've got to do an LP." I said, "What does that mean?" So he tells me he's got a whole bunch of new songs ready to go. Jumbo The Elephant, Pelican With the Broken Wing, another one for a rat. I said, "Chip, you've got the wrong man."

You know, I didn't get a penny out of it. I did it and the money all went to charity. I felt pretty good about that. I sing it once in a while. We held a fund raiser once and had a question and answer period during the event. One chap asked me, "Mr. Bower, you made a record, Honky The Christmas Goose?" I said, "Yeah." "Well, I've got that record." "Really?" I said. "You want to sell it? I'll give you $500."

He said, "I don't want to sell it, but how about you sing it?"
Now all of a sudden, there's about 150 people and they're
clapping their hands. So I sang a couple of lines and they're
all clapping, so I kept on going. Then, Joe Bowen, the Leafs
play-by-play man who was the emcee for the event, he said,
"Johnny, I think it's time for you to quit." I sang it the odd
time when they ask me to do it. The money was going to
charity and that's the only reason I did it.

It's very hard to find a copy of the record today and
when you do, I'm told you'll pay a fortune for it, so in case
you can't get one of your own, here's the words to the
song—Honky The Christmas Goose:

Honky, Honky the Christmas goose,
Got so fat that he was no use,
'till he learned how to blow his nose,
Honk! the way a goose nose blows.
After that and just for fun, it was a simple matter.
He would blow his honky horn to see the people scatter.
Cars and planes and trucks and trains, would get out of his way.
And when they heard that Honky horn, this is what they'd say,
Oh! Honky, Honky the Christmas goose,
Got so fat that he was no use,
'till he learned how to blow his nose.
Honk! the way a goose nose blows.
Christmas Eve was bright and clear,
no trouble was in sight.
But up in space a traffic jam gave Santa Claus a fright.
With rockets, kites and satellites and mice and dogs and all,
His team of tiny reindeer was slowed down to a crawl.
Oh! Honky, Honky the Christmas goose,
Got so fat that he was no use,
'till he learned how to blow his nose,
Honk! the way a goose nose blows.
Santa was sure worried for the children on his list.
He had to get a move on or their stockings would be missed.
Just then he heard a honky horn a coming down the sky.
And ev'rything moved over, to let the sleigh go by.
Oh! Honky, Honky the Christmas goose,

'tho he's fat, he is still some use.
Now he rides in the Christmas sleigh.
He honks his horn to tell the world
That Santa Claus is on his way
Honk!

The 1965-66 season was a real struggle for the Leafs. We were shutout in our first two games of the season and won just twice during our first nine games. We were fourth at mid-season, but picked up somewhat in the second half and climbed to finish in third place. I missed some time in February after suffering a 26-stitch cut during a practice session and also with a pulled hamstring. We used five goalies—Al Smith, Gary Smith and Bruce Gamble, besides Sawchuk and myself, but our goals against of 187 was second only to Montreal. We scored just 208 times, though, fourth-best in the league and the lowest of all the playoff teams.

The last game of the 1965-66 season in Detroit, we made a little bit of unusual history. I don't know what Punch was thinking, though. I started off in the first period and we were up 2-0. Then he pulled me out, telling everybody I had the flu and put Terry Sawchuk in net. After the second period, he pulled Sawchuk, insisting he'd tweaked his groin and put in Bruce Gamble. We were the first team to ever use three goalies in one NHL game, but it got even more bizarre. Punch told me to coach the third period and he took a seat a few rows up behind our bench. I said, "I can't put Gamble in and pull Sawchuk." I knew the rules and the third goalie could only play if the first two were both injured. He said, "Just do what you're told to do. I'll take care of it." Here's how Punch explained it to Paul Rimstead of the Toronto Globe & Mail. "Bower's sick . . . he's got the flu," Punch said. "Sawchuk felt a little pull in his groin and we didn't want to take any chances, so I declared an emergency situation." We ended up with a 3-3 tie. It was the first time I ever went behind the bench and all of the players wanted me to stay as coach instead of Punch, but I think Leaf fans probably disagreed, because we blew a 3-1 lead with me coaching.

First-place Montreal was our opponent in the playoffs and it wasn't a very pleasant experience. They whipped us in four straight games, the first time the Leafs had been swept since losing the 1959-60 Stanley Cup final to the same Canadiens.

As we headed into the 1966-67 season, a lot of the pre-season prognosticators were calling the Leafs a fifth-place club. There were about eight or nine guys on the team that were over 35 and they didn't give us a chance to win the Stanley Cup at all.

For much of the season, it looked like they'd be right. We won just one of our first six games, but were still in third place by the mid-season mark. But on January 15, 1967, we lost 4-0 at Chicago, the beginning of a club-record losing streak that would see us slide right out of our playoff position. A 5-2 home-ice loss to Detroit on February 8 was our 10th in a row, a new team mark. After the game, Frank Williams, a 20-year-old fellow from Kingston, Ontario who'd just returned from fighting in the Vietnam War, gave Punch a pin from his unit, the 101st United States Airborne Division. He was a Maple Leafs fan and he thought maybe it could bring us some luck. There were 68 men in his outfit when they were pinned down by the Viet Cong in Cam Rahn Bay. Williams was one of only three to make it out.

Maybe there was some luck in that pin, because we tied Chicago 4-4 in our next game, then went into Boston and beat the Bruins 2-1. The slump was over, but not for Punch. He was admitted to hospital in mid-February, suffering from exhaustion.

King Clancy actually took over as our coach for 12 games when Punch went into the hospital. He was the perfect medicine for what ailed us, an easy-going, effervescent presence in the room. We got on a roll under King, going 8-2-2, including a 3-0 win over Chicago March 4 that was Terry Sawchuk's record 100th NHL shutout. When Punch did come back on March 18, we had to play against Chicago, which was a pretty tough team, the first-place club. I thought he might wait for an easier game like New York, but he just fit back in like a glove. Everybody played their heart out and we won 9-5.

Punch's coaching tactics were different. We had a lot of fights in practice. Dickie Duff and Bobby Baun used to go at it quite a bit, but now we were getting mad and we were starting to play the way he wanted us to play. That's the way we would win games. We would scrimmage a lot. He felt that in scrimmaging, he could see everything that had to happen in a game. You'd do your skating drills, your shooting drills and scrimmage, scrimmage, scrimmage. The younger guys figured we practiced too long. Us older guys, it was good for us. We liked the work because we were older and it kept our legs loose.

We ended up in third place and would face the first-place Black Hawks in the semi-finals. In 1967, Chicago had a powerhouse. They should have won it. They ended up 15 points ahead of us. But we had the experience and the guys wanted to have their names engraved on the Stanley Cup one more time. I played my heart out. So did Tim Horton. So did Marcel Pronovost. So did Bobby Baun. The defense were a lot older than the guys up front. George Armstrong's legs were going, too, but he dug deep like the great leader he was. We all figured it was the last chance we were going to get to win the Stanley Cup.

Chicago won handily in the series opener 5-2, but we rallied for a 3-1 decision in Game 2, coming back to Maple Leaf Gardens all even. We were 3-1 winners in Game 3, but Chicago rallied for a 4-3 verdict in Game 4 and everything was even again as we returned to Chicago Stadium. Sawchuk had carried the load to this point because I'd broken a finger just prior to the playoffs, but Punch gave me the call to start Game 5. I got hurt and Sawchuk came in to start the second period with the scored tied 2-2. Well, the first shot Bobby Hull took on Terry Sawchuk dinged him right in the shoulder and he went down like he was dead. He got back up and played sensationally, though, stopping 37 shots as we won 4-

2. We took Game 6 by a 3-1 score and we were going on to the finals.

Punch told us before the series that if we beat Chicago, we'd win the Cup, because Montreal would be easy. Well, doesn't he go into Montreal and tell them they can't beat the Leafs with a junior B goalie, meaning Rogie Vachon, who was playing ahead of my old buddy the Gumper. Some of the things Punch said, I'll never know why he did. I guess he just believed in us that much.

Punch had funny ideas sometimes. One time we were playing Montreal in the playoffs and he had five defensemen out there right off the bat to start the game. I didn't know what he was doing. He's not matching lines, he was trying to disturb Montreal coach Toe Blake. He also liked to use his defensemen to take faceoffs in the defensive zone. Punch had somebody up there to keep stats on how many faceoffs we were losing in our own end and he was finding out that the defensemen weren't losing too many of them. I know I had a lot of confidence in them because he knew they were bigger and stronger and he wanted them to take the guy out and just leave the puck to lay there for a teammate to come and get it. A lot of the forwards we had couldn't do that because they weren't strong enough. It was Punch's theory and hey, it worked out pretty well.

Montreal hammered us 6-2 in the opener of the finals. I'd come in for Sawchuk to start the third period, then Punch went to me for Game 2. It was an afternoon game at the Forum and we blanked the Canadiens 3-0 as I turned aside 31 shots. They pelted me with 54 more pucks three nights later at Maple Leaf Gardens, but we were 3-2 winners when Bobby Pulford scored 8:26 into the second overtime period.

We could take a 3-1 stranglehold on home ice in Game 4, but the bad news was it was Thursday, April 27 and we were already 0-3 on Thursdays in the playoffs. Make that 0-4. We lost 6-2 and I didn't even get to see much of the game. I stretched a hamstring stopping a Larry Hillman drive during the warmup and when the game started, Sawchuk was in goal and Al Smith was on the bench as his back-up.

It stayed that way for Game 5 and we won 4-1 to take a 3-2 series edge. We could win it all back at the Gardens.

When I got to the rink the night of Game 6, I couldn't believe my eyes. I walked into the dressing room and right in the middle of the room, Punch had $10,000 in bills sitting there on a table. I went crazy. I looked and I'd never seen so many green leaves in all of my life. "Bower," Punch said. "This is how much money you can win if you beat Montreal tonight." I got up and he said, "Sit down. You're not coming any closer to this table until you win the Stanley Cup." Everybody just stared at it. That's the way Punch was. He was always thinking ahead, he always wanted to be ahead of the other guys. Some people might have looked at this idea as a joke, but it worked. I couldn't believe the money that we could have gotten. Of course, we didn't realize at the time that half of the money would go to the government in taxes. He even had a couple of guards in there watching the money and one of them seemed to be watching me pretty closely. I don't know why.

Before the game, Punch said to me, "How's your hamstring?" and I said, "It's pretty sore right now, but it should be okay." "Well," he said, "You're dressing." I wasn't anywhere near being okay. In fact, I could hardly put my pads on. Bobby Haggert, our trainer, had to tie the straps on my pads. I said, "It's useless for me to be on the bench."

But I sat there and I waited. On the ice before Game 6, there were three goaltenders out there for us—Smith, Sawchuk and myself. Punch said to me, "If anything happens, you'll have to go in. I said, "Okay, if I have to go in, I'll go in." The plan was that if it came to that, I'd go in, then fall down at the first chance and tell the ref I was injured. Al Smith was there, waiting in the dressing room. I don't know why Punch did it, but I'm thankful that he did it. He just wanted me to be there more than anything.

As it turned out, it didn't matter. Sawchuk was masterful and we won 3-1. The Stanley Cup was ours again. We'd beaten Montreal in six games, but boy, oh boy, if we had to play another game against Montreal, we wouldn't have made it. There were so many bruises. Red Kelly could hardly walk with a pulled groin. George Armstrong was all beat up. My body was all bruised up. I had bruises all over me. But we all knew that was probably going to be the last shot for all of us. It turned out great for us, but we suffered later on, because maybe Punch kept us too long.

People remember the old guys from that Maple Leafs team, but you can't forget the contributions made by the young players. In that final game against Montreal, it was Ron Ellis who gave us the lead and Jim Pappin and Pete Stemkowski who combined to create the eventual Cup winner.

Jimmy Pappin had a great series and scored a lot of big goals for us. Stemkowski was a big guy who'd go in the corner and forecheck. He was a good guy in the dressing room. I remember he'd never eat oranges in the dressing room. Everyone would eat oranges between periods, but he loved garlic sausage and had a piece of it all the time, he kept it underneath his bench in the dressing room. Punch would stalk around the room when he was having his meetings with us and always smelled something, but he couldn't figure out what it was. He found out later it was Stemkowski eating garlic sausage in the dressing room. Maybe that was a big factor for him, because Stemmer sure scared a lot of guys. He wanted to be a sports announcer more than anything and he ended up broadcasting for the San Jose Sharks.

Ronnie Ellis, I admired him. When he first came in, I used to work a lot with him after practice, took him under my wing. He worked well up and down the wing, he could skate, was a good checker, a good penalty killer and would get his share of goals. Great guy in the dressing room, but at first, he was very quiet, because he had to gather experience like everybody else. After a while, he started to loosen up a little bit and he turned out to be a great hockey player.

Another player who came up big for us in the playoffs that spring was Larry Hillman. He'd been up and down with us for years, but he really found his game playing on the defense alongside Marcel Pronovost. I don't think that pairing surrendered an even-strength goal the entire playoffs. He was an above average hockey player in my opinion, a good hockey player and a good guy.

Those players were a big addition to our club that season. Punch didn't make too many mistakes with his moves, the players he traded for and drafted. He just made a lot of mistakes getting rid of players that I liked.

CHAPTER NINE

A LEAF FOR LIFE

During our surprising run to the Stanley Cup in 1966-67, I think deep down, everybody in that Maple Leafs dressing room knew we were all part of something special and were enjoying a ride together that most of us would never take again as teammates.

Expansion was just around the corner. The National Hockey League was going to double in size from six to 12 teams to start the 1967-68 season and with so many players on our team over the age of 30, we knew many of us would be moving on at the end of the season. We all figured it was our last year to be Leafs. It's why we worked our hearts out to beat Chicago and Montreal.

We had a suspicion in the dressing room during that year that something like that was going to happen before the next season. That was one big factor in our success that spring. We all knew it was our last chance to do something significant together. I guess the team was talking about rebuilding, getting rid of the older players and bringing in some youngsters and that's what they did. They made a decision to go that way, because they knew the older players were going to go eventually anyway.

When the expansion draft was held—ironically on June 6, 1967, exactly 23 years to the day after D-Day—we were allowed to protect just one goaltender and 11 skaters. A lot of my teammates found out they'd be leaving Toronto. Terry Sawchuk, who was so sensational in goal for us during the 1967 playoffs went to the Los Angeles Kings. Red Kelly joined him there, retiring as a player to become the Kings' first coach, although Punch played hardball with Los Angeles. He reclaimed Kelly during the draft process and forced the Kings to make a trade to get Red's rights. Defenseman Bob Baun, who'd been with the Leafs since 1956, ended up going to the Oakland Seals, where he was named the first captain of the team. Oakland also took defenseman Kent Douglas and goalie Gary Smith. The Pittsburgh Penguins grabbed left-winger Larry Jeffrey, the St. Louis Blues took defenseman Al Arbour and the Philadelphia Flyers claimed left-winger Brit Selby, who'd been named NHL rookie of the year with us in 1965-66.

A couple of old guys who we didn't lose that day were defenseman Allan Stanley and my roomie, our captain George Armstrong. Neither of them were on our original protected list, but Punch was quick to claim them back. Each team was allowed to protect a player every time it lost a player during the draft.

Our original 11-player protected list looked like this—defensemen Tim Horton, Larry Hillman and Marcel Pronovost and forwards Mike Walton, Jim Pappin, Pete Stemkowski, Bob Pulford, Frank Mahovlich, Dave Keon, Ron Ellis and Brian Conacher and shockingly, me in goal. I was surprised when I was protected, but they had a lot of confidence in me, the coaching staff and the players who played in front of me, so I guess they made the right move.

One of our co-owners, Stafford Smythe, didn't seem so sure, though. At the expansion draft, he announced to the

Toronto papers, "I see that we protected our 47-year-old goalie." That was pretty good of Stafford to say that, but he forgot I was actually only 42.

We knew the changes were inevitable. We had a lot of veteran players in our lineup. Then finally, they had to leave. In fact, the majority of them were gone pretty quickly. By the beginning of the next season, Punch started to trade everybody away.

For the most part, Punch was very fortunate at making trades. It seemed every time he made a trade for somebody, he'd benefit. He was very lucky in cards and lucky in a lot of the things that he did. He was a good hockey man from the sense of knowing players. He did coach in the American Hockey League and spent a number of years with Boston. He had a good grasp on the talent of players. He knew who he wanted if the day ever came that he could get them.

Take me, for instance. He remembered me from Springfield. He told me once that the only reason they picked me up was because he remembered me beating his team and it wasn't because of the team in front of me, he felt I was the difference.

We started the 1967-68 season with several new faces in our lineup. Murray Oliver had come over from Boston in a trade for Eddie Shack. Forward Wayne Carleton and defenseman Duane Rupp were others who'd moved in as regulars and my new goaltending partner was Bruce Gamble.

I related to Bruce pretty easily, because he'd struggled like I did to make the big leagues. He was down in the minors for a long time. He'd had a couple of stints with us the previous two seasons and also chances with Boston and the New York Rangers, but this season, he finally made it for good. Bruce was a great guy, a great goaltender. He'd work hard in practice like I did. He'd never say anything in the way of a complaint, just hope to get in there and play a few games. If he didn't play and was sitting on the bench, he'd never say anything about it. I liked Bruce because in practice, I'd work hard at my end and he'd work hard down at his end and it would make it tough and that's what Punch liked, because we concentrated on defensive hockey.

Bruce was a guy who would get hurt and would still want to play. The padding that he was wearing was basically just his underwear and then some felt over his shoulders and the hard shots, when he got them from players who could really fire the puck like Bobby Hull, I'll tell you the next day, they'd really come up in a bruise. There were times there when he really should have pulled himself out of the net and said, "You know, I can't take it, I'm bruised pretty badly," but he wouldn't put another goaltender behind the eight ball. That's what I liked about Bruce and what everybody liked about Bruce. He was a good teammate.

Early in the season, we made our first West Coast road trip. When we would go to Los Angeles to play the Kings, a lot of Hollywood stars would come out for the games and some of them would come by the dressing room afterwards. One of them was Tiny Tim, who sang Tip Toe Through The Tulips, which was a big hit back then. He was a real Maple Leafs fan and he came in to meet the players. He shook your hand and it was just like shaking hands with a bowl of jelly. But the player he really liked on our team was Tim Horton. He went up to Timmy in that high-pitched voice of his and say, "Mr. Horton, you're my favorite player." Timmy was a pretty shy guy and he was really embarrassed by this.

We were scheduled to play in Oakland on Nov. 8, 1967, my 43rd birthday. They had a nice birthday cake for me and a bottle of champagne and it was quite a surprise to me, but we didn't touch that until after the game. Between the first and second period, they made a presentation at center ice and Barry van Gerbig, who was president of the Seals, presented me the cake with the bottle of champagne sticking out of the top of it. I told him that I'd counted the candles on the cake and there were only 42. Naturally, the Toronto Globe & Mail reported that I'd turned 44. Those reporters, they always had to try and make me older than I really was. I would have really enjoyed a shutout for my birthday, but as it turned out, we had a pretty good game and we beat them pretty handily by a 6-1 score. Murray Oliver and Jim Pappin each scored twice. I stopped 38 shots and drew an assist on a goal by Allan Stanley.

One thing I'd always wanted to do in the NHL but was never able to accomplish was to score a goal, although I came pretty close one time. We were playing against the New York Rangers one night. Gump Worsley was in goal and we were leading 2-1. The Rangers pulled the goaltender out and Bert Olmstead came tearing at me. I stopped the puck and I had a good, clear shot down the other end. And he said, "Shoot it, shoot it." So I shot it and I thought I was going to get my first goal. Actually, it was going right for the net, then it turned and missed by about six feet. I couldn't believe it. I got a little talking to from Bert afterwards. He said, "I didn't know you were such a bad shot." The next day at practice, all I did was practice long shots to see if I could score a goal, but it didn't pan out. That was the closest I ever got to scoring a goal. I got lucky enough to get a few assists here and there, but to get lucky enough to score a goal in the National Hockey League, that would have been a big feather in my hat, because at the time, it would have made me the first goalie ever to do it. With the curved stick now, of course, quite a few goalies have scored goals. As a team we struggled to score goals during the 1967-68 season. Our 209 goals were the lowest total of any of the so-called "Original Six" teams, which made it all the more strange that we opted to trade away our best goal scorer that season.

We were battling with the Chicago Black Hawks for the fourth and final playoff spot in the East Division and on March 3, 1968, Punch traded Frank Mahovlich, Garry Unger, Pete Stemkowski and the rights to Carl Brewer to the Detroit Red Wings for Norm Ullman, Floyd Smith, Paul Henderson and Doug Barrie. When they traded Frank it was a sad day for everybody and I thought Punch was nuts. I thought trading Frank was crazy. Punch explained his reasons for the trade to George Gross of the Toronto Telegram. "I think I improved the club for next season, otherwise I wouldn't have done it," he said. "If I stood still,

nothing could have improved. I got Norm Ullman for Pete
Stemkowski, or shall we say a 35-goal man for a 10-goal
center? Then I got Floyd Smith, a 24-goal performer, for
Garry Unger, who has yet to prove himself. He could
eventually become a good player, but we needed help
immediately. This brings us to Frank Mahovlich. Sure, he's a
better player than Paul Henderson. But Henderson is young
and could develop into a great star. Frank couldn't improve
with us in view of his health and hockey problems. The
change was the best thing to happen for him. He might return
to his previous form with Detroit. I hope so, for his sake."

Punch and Frank had their difficulties over the years.
They were at odds, no doubt about that. Frank had his
opinions about Punch and Punch had his opinions about
Frank. The trade, it was quite a surprise to everyone. In fact,
I remember coming home and telling Nancy I was going to
quit because they'd traded my best left winger. But that's
when George Armstrong came over and said, "You don't
want to pack it in over this. There's a lot of good players that
Punch is going to trade before this is all over. Whether you
like it or not, just play your own game and that's it." I said,
"But I liked Frank." And George said, "I know. Everybody
liked Frank. All the fans in Toronto loved Frank. But that's
none of your business. You've got a job to do and you just
have to go out there and do it." So he straightened me out.

We didn't straighten ourselves out, though. We missed
the playoffs, the first defending Stanley Cup champion to do
so since the 1945-46 Maple Leafs. The only saving grace
was our defensive play. Bruce Gamble and I finished with
just 176 goals against, second only to Montreal (168) in the
Vezina Trophy race. We nearly emulated Roy Worters of the
1930-31 New York Americans, the only goalie in NHL
history to post the lowest goals-against average on a team
that didn't make the playoffs.

When we arrived for training camp to start the 1968-69
season, there were more changes afoot. Jim Pappin had been
dealt to Chicago for Pierre Pilote, a Norris Trophy-winning
defenseman playing with the Black Hawks. Larry Hillman

was lost to Montreal in the intra-league draft and Allan Stanley went to Philadelphia in the reverse draft. In the 16 months since we'd won the Stanley Cup, 13 players from that team had departed.

"Winning the Stanley Cup was, possibly, the worst thing that happened to us," Punch explained to the Toronto Telegram. "I figured I had to give players on a winning team another chance. If I hadn't won the Stanley Cup, I would have made the changes then. This way, we've lost a year. "We've got eight players left from the championship team. Three of those may not make it and two could be traded."

The two Punch was thinking about trading were centers Bob Pulford and Mike Walton. Both would eventually be dealt, but not that season. Mike Walton didn't play too much for us, but he could shoot a puck and he'd score some goals for us when he did play. I don't think he got along too well with Punch. That was his own business, I don't know what it was. We'd bring him up and he'd play very well, then Punch would send him down. He didn't really give Mike a good chance to play for a long time. There was something about Shakey—that's what we called Mike—that Punch didn't like. I thought, "Hey, anytime we can bring up a young guy like that who can score goals—he even had a fight with Gordie Howe once and he held his own—why Punch didn't like him, I didn't know.

Now, the three guys Punch was ready to count out were Marcel Pronovost, George Armstrong and myself, but us old coots fooled him and made the team.

I was still popular in Toronto and was even starring in a television commercial for Muffets cereal. It was set up like a court room and I was in the witness box and I had my goal stick with me. I was being questioned by the prosecutor about how I could eat Muffets when I didn't have any teeth. "Mr. Bower is puck shy, your honor," he said. I smiled and they'd blacked out all my teeth. The judge asked how I could eat the Muffets? Then I said, "It's easy, they get soft when you add the milk."

We shut out Boston 2-0 early in the season on October 26 and it was a big deal for me, because shutting out the Bruins was no easy feat. They were the top-scoring team in the NHL and they had Bobby Orr. Bobby was a great offensive hockey player. I remember talking to the Gumper once about him and he said, "You know, that Bobby Orr, he controls the whole game." He could really handle the puck, he could shoot, he could stickhandle and he was not afraid or anything like that. He'd challenge you. If you wanted to come and try and check him, go ahead, but most of the time, he'd get away from the guy. Sure, he scored a few goals on me, but I got him a couple of times with the poke check. He was a great hockey player. His record speaks for itself. I thought he was great, but Gumper thought he wasn't great defensively. "You know us, we like our defensemen to stay back and play defense," Gumper would say. I guess Orr's coaches told him, "Look, if you can carry the puck up ice like that, you go ahead and do it."

Boston was one road city where I really enjoyed playing. The fans in Boston were super, just like in Toronto. If you worked hard and gave it a good, solid effort, they'd give you a lot of credit. But if you didn't work hard and give it that extra push, they'd give you a hard time. Not playing for them and not wearing that Bruins uniform, I still got a good ovation there every so often. I got a shutout there one night and I think I must have stopped 50 shots, so they gave me a standing ovation.

The 1968-69 season was also a unique one for me, because it was the season I finally relented and put on a goal mask. I never liked masks. When I was kid going to public school in Prince Albert, I played a little baseball. I was the catcher, but I didn't like a mask at all, so I went behind there without it. To be honest, I only got hit a couple of times on top of the head with foul tips. After a short time, though, I came to my senses and thought, "Hey, I better start wearing a mask."

It didn't happen so quickly in hockey, but after nearly a quarter-century of facing pucks bare-faced, it finally happened. One night, Punch pulled Gamble out of the net and he put me in. I really didn't want to go in, because Bruce was playing well and at the time, I think we had a six-goal lead for the Vezina Trophy. I guess maybe Punch didn't want us getting that $1,000 bonus for winning the Vezina. As he put me in, he said, "From now on, you've got to wear a mask." I wore it for 17 games in the regular season, but I never did like it. I'd used one in practice for years. In Cleveland I used one that was a clear fiberglass mask simply for protection to keep me from getting cut or hurt . When I went to Toronto, I kept wearing it, but I didn't like the looks of it. Punch told me I'd better go to Boston and get one made like the rest of the goalies were doing at the time.

Down the street from me lived our family dentist, Dr. Ric Bell and he was the one who made my first mask for me. I liked it in a way. It was a color similar to my skin and I started to get used to it, but the eyes were fairly small. They had to be so the puck wouldn't go through. There was a spot there around my feet where I couldn't see the puck and I was depending on my defensemen to help me out in that instance. I wasn't happy or pleased with the mask at all. I just felt it was slowing me down. It gives you a lot of confidence, there's no doubt about that. Today there's almost no way a goaltender can get hurt while wearing a mask. I could feel the shots in practice, there's no doubt about that. That's why I put it on, because a lot of times, I'd get a little nick over the eye, so it was a big help in practice, but I didn't really like wearing the mask in the games.

We rebounded from our miss the previous season and grabbed fourth place, the final playoff spot. We'd meet the second-place Bruins in the quarter-finals. I didn't know it for sure at the time, but this would be my final Stanley Cup series, so I'd come full circle. My first NHL playoff round was in 1959 against the same Bruins.

We'd won that set in seven games, but this one wouldn't be nearly as enjoyable. We went down to Boston for the first two games and got hammered 10-0 and 7-0. The first game was the night that Pat Quinn put Bobby Orr out for the game with a big hit, touching off a brawl-filled encounter. Johnny McKenzie started it with Forbes Kennedy. Two little midgets started it all going. We had a quite a night, everybody was fighting. It was a good one, both teams poured off the benches and went at it. It was quite a battle. The 38 combined penalties and our 20 penalties were both Stanley Cup records. Kennedy also set four playoff records—most penalties in a game (eight), most penalty minutes in a game (38), most penalties in a period (six) and most penalty minutes in a period (34). He also got suspended four games for striking referee John Ashley. As the battle raged, I skated out from my crease. Then Boston goalie Gerry Cheevers, started out from his net and we met at center ice and started talking. The two of us had the best seat in the house to watch the fights. Everybody thought we were yapping at each other, but we were just talking about watching the other players fighting. We were saying, "Look at these stupid guys. Fighting, grabbing each other, going crazy. They've got to be out of their minds." Goaltenders don't fight. We're all lovers.

The series shifted to Maple Leaf Gardens and while we put up a better display, the Bruins still swept us, taking 4-3 and 3-2 decisions. I came in to replace Bruce Gamble to start the second period of Game 3 and was chosen second star after stopping 28 shots and got the start in Game 4. At 44 years, four months and 28 days, I'm the oldest goalie ever to appear in a Stanley Cup game.

After it was over, my old pal Cheesy, who I'd worked with all those years ago in Toronto when he first broke into the league, he offered me some flattering words. "It was a thrill for me just to have sat beside him," Cheevers told the Toronto Telegram. "He's so great and has been for so long. He always gave 100 per cent and he did against us."

The news got worse after we were eliminated, when Stafford Smythe announced that Punch Imlach had been fired as coach-GM. They said he was going to be fired in the papers, but it just seemed every time we didn't win the Stanley Cup or an important game, they were going to fire the coach. I was sad to see Punch go, because I got along well with him. I was hurt inside when it happened. He was the one who gave me the opportunity and the chance to be with an NHL club in 1958-59. I told everyone after the game that I was going to retire. I said, "I can't go on any further, no matter who the coach might be that came in." George Armstrong came to me and said, "Just hold on. It'll be okay. Another year won't hurt. You're going to get paid and you're finally making a little bit of money now, so you might as well stay and do the best you can. Maybe we can win another Stanley Cup together before you go." But it didn't turn out that way.

Nonetheless, Chief convinced me to come back for the 1969-70 season. Jim Gregory was our new GM and interestingly, John McLellan, the guy who'd hit me with that backhand shot in the face that January 1953 night so many years ago in Pittsburgh, was the new coach of the Maple Leafs. Toronto opted to go with three goalies that season— myself, Bruce Gamble and Marv Edwards, who we'd picked up from Pittsburgh. I didn't care for it too much. Not that I didn't like the guys—both Brucie and Marv were great guys—the reason why was that I needed that extra work. I thrived on hard work and I just felt that putting somebody else in there would take away 15-20 minutes to a half an hour of work away from me, which I needed badly. The three goaltender system to me never did work and never will work. I told John McLellan that many times. "I need more work. I can't get enough work in practice to keep in shape." I didn't go along with it at all, but I had no alternative, so I dealt with it.

I turned 45 November 8, 1969 and that was a historic day for me and hockey. At 45, you qualify to receive your NHL pension and I became the first National Hockey Leaguer to be an active player and eligible to collect my pension at the same time. But I didn't claim it. I was saving that money for when I retired. Bruce and Marv carried the load early in the season, but then Marv injured his knee in November and on December 10, 1969, I got the call to make my first start of the season at the Montreal Forum against the Canadiens. "What the heck, this is my hunch and I'm going to go with it," McLellan told Dan Proudfoot of the Toronto Globe & Mail. I hadn't played since our Blue and White game October 7 at the end of training camp and I was really shaky there for awhile. On top of that, we had six players on the injured list. Forwards Paul Henderson and Dave Keon were out, as were four regular defensemen—Pat Quinn, Rick Ley, Mike Pelyk and Brian Glennie. The defensive corps in front of me that night against the defending Stanley Cup champion Habs consisted of Tim Horton, Jim Dorey, Jim McKenny, Marcel Pronovost, who'd been recalled from Tulsa, where he was coaching our farm team and Chris Evans and Gord Nelson, two rookies who were making their NHL debuts. When you get a couple of rookies up like that, you try your best to get them to relax. I told them to just play their game and they did. They did a good job, considering they put them in there cold. Although I had confidence in these kids, things were pretty scary there for awhile. I knew I'd have to be sharp on every shot that Montreal would take. And Montreal took a lot of shots. I stopped all 14 the Canadiens aimed at me in the first period and McKenny gave us a 1-0 lead. It was 3-2 for us after two periods, then the roof fell in and we lost 6-3. Claude Provost completed the scoring with an empty-net goal. They pelted me with 15 third-period shots. I couldn't blame the rookies. We lost because of the injuries that we had and bad goaltending.

At least I can say the first and last goals I ever allowed in the NHL were scored by Hockey Hall of Fame defensemen. Serge Savard was the last one to beat me that night in Montreal and back on October 8, 1953, it was Red Kelly who scored the first one on me.

No one realized it at the time, but that performance in Montreal would be my last as an National Hockey Leaguer. I continued to dress as Bruce Gamble's back-up for the next seven games, including a pair against the New York Rangers where myself and Terry Sawchuk, the goalies for Toronto's 1967 Stanley Cup win, were the opposite No. 2 netminders.

At practice December 29, I hurt my knee and they sent me to the hospital. It was a strange day in the Bower household, because while I was being checked into Toronto's Wellesley Hospital, our daughters Barbara and Cindy were getting out of Humber Hospital after having their tonsils removed.

I didn't want to go out of the lineup at all, because once I missed a few games, it was hard for me to get back into shape. I had to stay out and do all kinds of extra work on the ice. Do my stops and starts, the circles, even after everybody was gone. But I just had to do it because of my age. I think I set a good example for the younger guys. They'd wonder how come I was always the last guy on the ice at practice every day and I'd say, "Well, it's hard work, but you only get what you put into it." I wanted to stay in Toronto for as long as I could. As long as the players and the management had confidence in me, I was okay.

And they seemed to still believe in me. "We're very disappointed," Maple Leafs GM Jim Gregory told the Toronto Globe & Mail after my injury. "We planned to use Bower in the next few games to give Bruce Gamble a rest." Instead, the Leafs signed Gerry McNamara from the Orillia Terriers seniors to fill my spot, the same goalie who'd replaced me when I'd hurt my groin back in 1961.

I tried to come back from my knee injury, but things just weren't going my way. I came home one day and I told Nancy, "I can't go on any longer. I'm letting in a lot of long shots in practice that I shouldn't be and I think it could be because my eyes are going." She agreed with me. There would be a spot for a young guy and they were going to start rebuilding with youngsters. Then she said, "What are you going to do?" I said, "Well, I went to see Mr. Gregory and they had something planned for me."

I officially announced my retirement on March 19, 1970. It was difficult giving up a game I'd played professionally since 1945, but even though I was leaving the ice, there was still an opportunity in hockey for me. The Leafs were going to make me a scout and a goalkeeping coach. I didn't feel too badly about bowing out as a player and I felt a whole lot better about it when Mr. Gregory offered me the job with the organization.

I would no longer wear the Toronto uniform, but I was going to be a Maple Leaf forever.

CHAPTER TEN

THERE IS LIFE AFTER HOCKEY

Making the transition from playing after stopping pucks for a quarter-century was a challenge, but I think it was worse for Nancy than me, because now when we went to a game, she was the one coming home all bruised up.

We used to get two passes to Maple Leaf Gardens every time there was a hockey game, so Nancy and I would go to the game. When I first retired, I used to sit with her a few times and when I say a few times, it was a few times, because my reflexes were still there and when a goaltender would make a great save, out would come my arm and I'd get Nancy in the ribs. She wasn't too happy about that. Finally, she told me to go sit up in the press box. I sat with her a couple of more times, but after that, it was the press box for me and she would bring a friend or one of the children to sit with her in the seats.

I was adapting to my new career with the Leafs. I liked scouting, because you got to travel all over and meet a lot of different people. I know it was tiresome when I would go away on a 15-day trip from coast to coast, but you got to look at a lot of talent and some great young hockey players. I went to Charlottetown on one of my first scouting trips and found Errol Thompson. Here's a young kid, 19 years old, playing senior hockey in Charlottetown, P.E.I. He could skate and shoot a puck and he had a backhand shot that I couldn't believe. He was playing with these old guys and I thought that was strange. We had a part-time scout out there at the time and I asked him about it. He said, "These guys out here, they don't want to leave. Once they get away from home, they get a little lonely and get homesick. I've talked to him many times, but maybe you might have some success." I went over and I saw him after a game. I told him, "I thought you played a tremendous game." Errol said, "I have a lot of fun with these guys, no question at all. I enjoy the game and I've got a good job. I'm happy doing what I'm doing." At the time, he was working at a gas station pumping gas.

I said, "Hey listen. I've got to file a report on you because I think you've got the talent and I really feel you've got the skating legs to play pro, but there's one thing. Do you mind me telling you something?" He said, "No" and I said, "I think you're a little bit overweight." He said, "Well, you know, we don't drink Coke in the dressing room after the game. Our pop is supplied by a brewery." I said, "Fine, I understand, but if Toronto were to draft you, would you come?" He said, "Maybe." "Well," I said, "If you do come, how much do you weigh?" He said, "I weigh 218." "You're five-foot-nine and you weigh 218 and you can move around the ice like you do?" I said. "Boy, that's a big asset." But I said, "You've got to do me a big favor. If we do draft you, could you please come into camp maybe weighing about 200 pounds?" He was a little startled. "Wow, you mean I've got to lose that much weight?" he said. "Well, it's up to you, really," I said. "I'm out here to scout you and I've got to put a report in on you, because I think you're good enough to make it." He didn't say anything, just sort of smiled and that was it.

When we got to the table for the draft meetings (in 1970), I think we got him in the second round. Bob Davidson, Toronto's chief scout, came up to me and I said, "Bob, we're into the second round and Errol Thompson is still there. We've got to take him. He's better than some of the guys that have already been picked." He said, "You've got to be kidding me." I said, "I'm telling you Bob, this kid can skate. He's not the biggest guy, but he can keep up with anybody in our league. And he can shoot." He said, "Are you sure?" And I said, "I am sure about it. I know it. After looking at George Armstrong all those years and the way he could skate, I'm telling you this kid could skate rings around George Armstrong." Anyway, we picked him in the second round. Mr. Stafford Smythe, the Leafs' co-owner, is sitting at the table, it's my first year scouting and he looks at me and says, "You just put your job on the line." I figured, "Uh, oh."

I phoned Errol and told him we'd drafted him and I said, "When you come to training camp, don't forget what I told you." And he promised, "Mr. Bower, I won't forget." When Errol came to training camp, he got on the scale and was at 208. I figured he'd made a pretty good effort for me. I saw a little bit of heart there that showed me he wanted to play for us. He came into training camp and boy he played well. Then Lanny McDonald came and Darryl Sittler and what a line that was for us. Errol scored 43 goals for the Leafs in 1975-76. I see Errol every once in a while and I say, "I took you away from home, but boy, I made a millionaire out of you, didn't I?"

I enjoy telling stories like that, but I don't like doing speaking engagements. I love doing question and answer sessions, though. People want to ask questions. They give you some good questions and I enjoy answering them. And they go home happy.

They want to know about Punch, what kind of coach was he. Did you have any arguments with other players? Sure, a lot of times I got mad at my defensemen and a lot of times, they got mad at me. But most of all, they want to know about Mr. Ballard.

I know a lot of people have a lot of different things to say about Harold Ballard, who owned the Leafs for most of the time I worked as a scout for the team. All I can talk about is how he was with me and most of the time, he treated me great. Although he did fire me once.

That was quite a deal. I was on the road for a couple of weeks and when I came back, I was sitting at my desk and Mr. Ballard came along and said, "Where have you been?" "Out west, Mr. Ballard," I told him. "See any good hockey players out there?" he asked and I said, "Oh yeah, quite a few." "We're going to get them all, right?" he asked. And I said, "No, we can't get them all." "What do you mean we can't them all?" he demanded. "I said, "Well, it depends on where we end up in the standings and who's available in the draft." "Who made those rules?" he wanted to know. Well actually, I was ready to tell him that he was one of the ones who was responsible for making those rules, but I was afraid to say so, because he was my boss.

Anyway, he went on and he kept saying, "You know, I'm sick and tired of you guys. You scouts told me how good Lanny McDonald was. For two years, I've paid him a good salary and he's done nothing for me." I said, "Mr. Ballard, he came right out of junior hockey. It takes a couple of years sometimes to develop these kids." "I'm not waiting two years," he snapped. "I'm in a business here and I can't do that. You know, all you scouts, all you do is give me a headache. I've got a notion to fire everybody." Then he said, "In fact, you're fired." I said, "Okay."

So I took all my papers that I had on my desk and I had a box there that I was putting all my stuff in, my personal stuff and the things I had on top of my desk and George Armstrong comes in and he says, "What are you doing?" I said, "I just got fired." "What did you say to Mr. Ballard?" George asked me. And I said, "I don't know what I said to him, George, but I know one thing. He fired me." Then I said to George, "You know, in fact, you're the guy who should be fired, because you liked McDonald more than anybody." Now he started to laugh and giggle, but it wasn't funny, it sort of hurt me inside. So I said to him, "You know, this isn't funny, George," but he's still laughing. Then finally, he said to me, "Put your stuff back on the desk and go home." So I did that. I put my stuff back on the desk and everything and I said to George, "Are you sure?" and he said, "Just do what you're told."

Well, I'll tell you, I didn't sleep at all that night. I was really worried. I had a wife and three kids at home and I needed that scouting job. I came back the next morning at 10 o'clock and the first thing I heard coming toward me was that shuffle that everyone at Maple Leaf Gardens knew was Mr. Ballard's walk. And there he was, right in front of me. And he looked at me and said, "Good morning, John, how are you?" I said, "Fine, Mr. Ballard." He didn't even remember that he'd fired me. I couldn't believe it. When it was all over with, George Armstrong came over to me and said, "Well, I see you're still at your desk." I said, "Yeah." Then I said, "Tell me something. What was so funny about Mr. Ballard firing me. I'm married, I've got three kids, you know that George." And he said, "You really want to know?" I said, "Yes, I definitely would like to know." So he says, "All right, I'll tell you. He's fired me six times." I said, "Why didn't you tell me that? I couldn't sleep all night long." Anyway, it turned out I still had my job.

In 1972, I had a chance to return to playing and go to the WHA. The New England Whalers approached me. They wanted me to come out of retirement and play. I talked to Nancy and she said, "No. You worked too hard to establish your reputation in the NHL to go to the WHA. They've treated you well in Toronto. It was your ambition to do what you wanted to do and you've completed it. I'd advise you to stay put." So I had to listen to her and I stayed put. And I'm glad I did, because the league only lasted seven years before the last four teams merged with the NHL.

I was enjoying what I was doing, anyway. I liked working with goalies. I think everybody should have a goalie coach. It's pretty hard when you think about it. Suppose you're a goalie coach for Martin Brodeur. This guy is one of the best goaltenders in the game, he's got his own style, but like anybody else, he's going to have his good days and his bad days. It's pretty hard to teach a goalie, but if he respects you, he'll come to you. That's what I used to do. Mike Palmateer and I would sit down and I'd say, "Michael, how do you feel?" Then he might say, "I let in that goal the last game and did you notice what I did wrong?" He was asking me questions and that's what I wanted him to do. Then I could say, "Well, you went out too fast," or, "You could have used your poke check there," or, "The puck went through the crease area and you could have deflected the shot away from the net." Whatever questions he'd ask me, we'd talk, then he'd say, "Good, thank you" and that was it. You can't go right at a goaltender, you've got to wait for him to come to you. That's the way I got along with all of the Leafs goaltenders over the years. I'd let them know, "I'm not here to criticize you, I'm here to help you as much as I possibly can." It turned out pretty good for me.

When I was in town, a lot of times I would go on the ice and work with the goaltenders. If one of the goaltenders got hurt, they'd call me and say, "John, you've got to practice with the team." It was like that for quite a while. I wasn't moving too fast at that time at my age, but hey, I was better than putting a chair in there.

On January 9, 1980, I almost made a comeback at the age of 55. Both of the Maple Leafs goalies were out—Palmateer was nursing an ankle injury and Paul Harrison had the flu. I was the only guy in Toronto who wasn't sick or hurt. Punch Imlach, who came back as the Leafs GM in 1979, he decided, "I've got to do something." I was in pretty good shape because I was still practicing with the goalies, so I was taking a few shots here and there. Vince Tremblay was recalled from Moncton of the American League to start and the plan was that I'd dress as the back-up. Floyd Smith was the Leafs' coach at the time and he told the press that if I dressed, I was going to play at least part of the game. I thought, "Boy, oh boy, wait until these young guys find out I'm going to make a comeback." Punch got the contract out and I signed it for one dollar and he said, "Make sure you're here on time." Well, when I got to the dressing room, Tremblay was there and Palmateer was all better. I guess they didn't want me to come in, but I was all ready to go back in. I got there around 6 o'clock, got in the dressing room, took my coat off and saw Palmateer in there. I went into the medical room where Punch was and he said, "Don't go away. Hang around, just in case." So I stayed around the dressing room and I watched most of the game on TV. I was sitting in there, with my skates on, to get used to them in case they needed me. But nothing happened. Good thing it didn't, I probably would have gotten bombed, but you never know. I've seen goalies go in when the regular goalie gets hurt and the team plays their hearts out in front of them. I think if I had gone in, I would have been going to church, lighting a lot of candles, because I would have been playing against Montreal, the defending Stanley Cup champions. I wasn't scared or anything like that. If I had gotten a shutout, maybe I would have gotten a little more money from Punch.

One goalie I remember working with who was a real challenge for me was Jiri Crha. George Gross actually was the one who saw him play. A Toronto newspaperman, he was overseas and he saw this kid Crha playing in the Czech League. He got a hold of Punch, because they were good friends and told him, "There's a good, tall Czech kid playing goal over here. He's still developing, but he's going to be a good one, if you can get him out." That was a big problem, but they managed to get him out and Punch sent me to the airport. "I want you to go pick up this kid," he said. "How will I know him?" I asked. "You'll know him by the cap he'll be wearing," Punch said. "And he won't be wearing expensive clothes." So I go to the airport and I'm sitting there waiting. He could hardly speak English and I said to him, "Is your name Crha?" and he nodded. We shook hands. I brought him back to Punch's office and we sat there with George Gross, who was Czech and could translate everything I said to Crha.

George told him, "Mr. Imlach wants you to work with Mr. Bower. He's going to help you out in goal." He seemed to understand. Everything went fine for awhile. When the season started and we went to training camp, I said, "George," because that's what we called Crha, "You know you're letting the puck go around the boards. You should stop it behind the net and set it up for your defensemen." He said, "No," and shook his head. So I told him to watch what I'm going to do. He said, "No, no, I can't go." I had to get George Gross and I found out later that the reason why he wouldn't do it was because he'd been told not to do it because overseas, the area behind the net to the back boards was so much deeper than what it is in the NHL. If you get caught behind the net there, it's a goal for sure. So he was taught to stay in the net and here I was, trying to teach him to go out.

Eventually, he learned before it was all over to get out there and stop it. He played one game I remember against Minnesota. I think we lost 1-0 and he stopped about 55 shots. After that, though, things didn't turn out for him.

Now Palmateer, he was exactly the opposite. Whatever came into his mind, he'd go right after the guy. He'd leave his net and he'd get them most of the time. Michael was a good, young goalkeeper with Toronto. We had a few of them like that over the years and when they traded these young goaltenders, it was pretty sad to see them go, because you'd work with them and teach them and then you'd hope they would stay for 10-12 years.

One of the nice things about retiring as a player was that I got to spend so much more time with my family. The family of a hockey player makes so many sacrifices to make his career go more smoothly, that it's nice to be able to return the favor.

One of the perks was being able to take Nancy to Hawaii for our 25th wedding anniversary. It was really something when we decided to go to Hawaii. We had a great time. We had a ball. The scenery was just beautiful. We both needed a holiday and we really enjoyed it there. I loved Maui and I love Hawaiian music. We had a bus driver who was originally from Canada and he had a great voice. He would sing songs for us to pass the time. To this day, Nancy still wants to go back to Hawaii. Above all, she had a good holiday and she deserved one.

Another activity I strive to be part of every day is that I do help out Nancy a lot around the house with the housework. Now maybe you fathers are going to get mad at me, but I'll tell you, it's good exercise to get that mop going, pushing it back and forth. The vacuuming is another area I like to help with. That's heavy to push for her so I enjoy helping her with the housework. I do a lot of sweeping here and there and I even help make the beds. I can make a bed perfectly, with no wrinkles in it at all. I like doing things like that. Maybe that's why my marriage has lasted, for 57 years, because I like to help her. We work together and that makes married life so much easier. You dads should be helping out around the house and doing the dishes once in a while, give your wives a break.

I learned that lesson when I was playing in Cleveland. Jim Hendy, our owner, one time when we won the Calder Cup, he called the wives in. We had a little paycheck coming and he made the checks out to the wives instead of the players. It was for about $400-$500, which was a lot of money at the time. He said, "The wives deserve something like that, because after all, they take care of you guys and keep you ready to play."

We have a great family with our children Johnny, Barbara, and Cindy and including our two grandsons, John III and Bruce and our four granddaughters, Staci, Kelly, Dale and Alison. I'm very proud of all of them.

John II and his wife Janice live in Calgary, where he's a team leader in Environment, Health and Safety and Operations Support for Petro Canada. We miss him a lot, mind you, but he's worked hard for it. He strives on hard work as well. He had a brief pro hockey career, too.

He was a defenseman and in 1974, the Washington Capitals drafted him. He went to training camp and he didn't do too badly. He had some problems with his skating, but he had a good head on his shoulders, he passed the puck well, had a good shot and was pretty tough. He was sent down to the American Hockey League to training camp with Springfield, which was Eddie Shore's team. That's the same Eddie Shore who tried to sign me to a pro contract back in 1945.

I was surprised that Mr. Shore accepted such an inexperienced player, but he did. "Mr. Shore," John was telling me, "he never went on the ice, but he'd pace up and down an area along the boards and watch everybody." All of a sudden, he'd blow the whistle and say, "Mr. Bower, you are not lifting your legs when you are skating backwards. You should lift them up a little higher." And while he's talking, he's demonstrating how it should be done. And Johnny said, "You know dad, I'm starting to learn a lot about hockey from that man." Eddie Shore was a great hockey player in his day. He was tough and that's why he won a lot of hockey games.

Eddie Shore also helped me out during my playing days. I met him when I was in the AHL and he said, "You've got a few bad scars there. You know what you should do? Go buy some cocoa butter and keep rubbing it on your scars every day. When you've got nothing to do, when you're watching TV or you're sitting down having a Coke, keep rubbing it and rubbing it and eventually, they'll go away." And you know what? A lot of my scars did go away. He was scarred up, too, in his day when he played, but you didn't really notice a lot of them.

I've had over 200 stitches in my face. Most of my injuries occurred in practice more than games, because you tend to let up a little bit in practice. I didn't move like I should be moving and I'd get one in the lip or around the eye. I'm actually very fortunate that I never did lose an eye, because the deflections in practice, they could get you.

John's son is also named John and that tends to cause a lot of confusion when we get the family together. Nancy would call, "John" and we'd either all show up, or say,

"Which one?" So Nancy came up with a solution. I became JB I, my son John became JB II and his son, my grandson John, became JB III.

Barbara is a customer service coordinator and a recovery specialist for SunGard Recovery Systems. They provide back-up data systems for some of the world's largest companies and can retrieve information when it's lost. They did a lot of work recovering computer records for companies that were housed in the World Trade Center following the September 11, 2001 terrorist attacks.

Cindy operates her own power skating school and she's done very well for herself. She's had quite a number of NHL players come through her program. Rick Tocchet was one of her first students. She's worked with the Philadelphia Flyers and Edmonton Oilers. She's involved in a hockey school now with Adam Bennett, who played in the National League with Chicago and Edmonton until he got hurt and had to retire. Occasionally, Cindy phones me and says, "I've got a private lesson for you. You want to come up and take it?" "Okay fine, I'll come up and take it," I usually tell her.

For 20 years, John II, Cindy and I operated the Johnny Bower Goaltending School for young goalies. It was a lot of fun and we got to work with some great young goalies, both boys and girls. It was a really family-oriented operation, because my grandsons John III and Bruce and Cindy's husband Bruce also worked as instructors at the school.

Two of my most famous students were John Vanbiesbrouck, who won the Vezina Trophy in 1985-86 and two-time NHL all-star Curtis Joseph. Curtis was one of my students for a long time and I like to tell a story about him. He came to my school and he was a reflex goaltender—he still is today—and he depends on his feet, did the butterfly and he kept going down all the time. I said, "CuJo, if you don't learn to stand up and challenge the shooter, you're going to have a lot of problems as you move along in hockey." And he said, "It's not my style. I go down like that. It's the way I play." I told him, "I want you to come out and challenge the shooter," but he said, "If I come out too far, I

get lost. If I'm in that crease area, I know where I am."
"Well," I said, "it's nice to know two ways instead of one
way." And he said, "Yeah, you're right." So I got him to
stand up a little bit more. Other times, he'd go down, but he
was learning. At least he was trying, which was the main
thing.

He wasn't drafted by the OHL and decided to go to Notre
Dame in Saskatchewan and from there on he did very well. I
picked up the paper and saw he'd been signed by St. Louis
and I thought, "Oh, no," but I told Nancy he probably
wouldn't remember what I said. Anyway, he played pretty
well for St. Louis and years later when he was a free agent,
Toronto grabbed him and I thought, "Oh, this is going to be
fun." He got into Toronto and I went up to him, shook his
hand, congratulated him and wished him the best of luck. He
said, "Mr. Bower, remember the time you said that I would
never make the National Hockey League if I didn't stand up
more?" And I said, "Yes, I did. How did you remember
that?" And he said, "Oh, I remember." So I said, "Well, I'm
sorry I said that, but maybe it was a good lesson that I gave
you and I'll tell you one thing—I made a millionaire out of
you and I'm still waiting for a check." He's a good kid, a
fine fellow. I still like CuJo to this day.

Two years ago, we stopped the goalie school. I thought it
was finally time to give it up. I enjoyed it so much working
with the kids who were just starting out, but I was getting up
in age. When you get on that ice, you've got to work hard. I
had to try and keep up with them, teach them the poke check,
how to play the angles.

I ran the goalie school for the same reason I do a lot of
charity work, because I enjoy meeting people. It's very
educational. It's good to know these people and they're good
hockey fans. It's an education for me, too, to listen to what
the people have to say. A couple of years ago, I was made an
honorary police chief for Peel Region in Ontario. I asked for
one of their cruisers, but they wouldn't go that far. But I did
get a uniform. In 2000, I was presented the Mel Osborne
Fellowship by the Kiwanis Club of Credit Valley, Ontario,

an award which honors people for their contribution to the community. That was a great honor, because I was just the second person outside the Kiwanis Club to receive the award. The first was actor Roger Moore, who played James Bond in the movies.

I like playing in charity golf tournaments. Golfing is wonderful. It's very frustrating for me at times when I'm not playing well. I'm not what you'd call a great golfer, I'm usually around 92 or 93, but I love mixing up with the people. I like to have a lot of fun. It costs nothing for a smile. It doesn't hurt anybody if you smile and say, "Hi, how are you?" It's not that hard.

Years ago, when I was doing an autograph signing at a Tim Horton's in Brantford, apparently one of the youngsters I signed for that day became pretty famous in his own right. It was Wayne Gretzky. Wayne mentioned it to me once and told me mine was the first autograph he'd ever gotten from anyone. I have to honestly say that I can't recall Wayne. He was a little guy then. At the time, nobody knew he was going to turn out to be the great star that he is, an ambassador to hockey. He got my autograph that day with his father Walter. I see his father quite often. I've appeared in his charity golf tournament. I have to say yes to Walter. He's such a great guy and he does so much work for charity, you can't say no to Walter. When I'm not doing charity work or spending time with my family, my other passion is fishing. Gordie Howe and I used to go fishing out west. He's a lucky guy. He'd always catch more fish than I would. I had the hotel and the coffee shop in Waskesiu and he'd come up and work on the golf course at Prince Albert National Park. We got to know each other very well.

I love fishing. I think it's very relaxing. Every August, we go to a place just north of Vancouver and we catch salmon galore. There's about six of us hockey players that go each summer. We have a great time there. It's a lot of fun.

There's also great fishing at our cottage. Not long after I joined the Maple Leafs, I went to the Toronto Sportsmen's Show. I was walking around and they had these nice-looking cottages all set up. I thought, "Wouldn't it be nice to have one of those?" We didn't really want to go too far. The woman at the booth selling the cottages said, "We have a place called Bobcaygeon and there's a lot of property being developed up there—Pigeon Lake, Little Bald Lake and Big Bald Lake. "Is there good fishing?" I asked and she said, "Oh yes, very good fishing up in that area." I got all the information, we studied the area and we bought a piece of property on Little Bald Lake and we put up a cabin and we've been there close to 40 years.

It's still standing really well and we've got a couple of little bunkies where the kids come in on weekends. We have a lot of fun. It's so relaxing. I love the fresh air. I can go up there and take it easy. Putting around, there's always something to do when you have a cottage. We built quite a bit of it ourselves. The framework was done by the carpenters. The inside work and the additions, we did that ourselves. It's a good-sized cottage and can sleep about 10 people.

Next to winning the Stanley Cup, my greatest thrill in the game came in 1976, when I was inducted into the Hockey Hall of Fame. What a great honor that was. I didn't think I'd get inducted into the Hockey Hall of Fame. I couldn't believe it. It's so hard to explain the feeling. I was just dumbfounded. In fact, I broke down. I waited for six years to get in, but what a happy thrill for me and Nancy and our whole family. What a great feeling. Your whole body goes numb. It's something I'll never forget.

I know there's no way I would have gone into the Hall of Fame if it wasn't for the team that Punch put in front of me—Horton, Stanley, Brewer, Baun, George Armstrong, Pulford, Ronnie Ellis, Frank Mahovlich—just to name a few. Man, oh man, I was so thankful for those guys because I always maintain that a goalie is only as good as the people in front of him. Sure, you have to do your job, but they're out there to help you as well.

Another great thrill came early in 2006, when I was selected among the inaugural class to be inducted into the

AHL Hall of Fame. I joined Jack Butterfield, Jody Gage, Fred Glover, Willie Marshall, Frank Mathers and Eddie Shore in this elite group and we were all honored during the AHL All-Star festivities in Winnipeg.

I'm actually enshrined in nine different halls of fame—the Hockey Hall of Fame, the AHL Hall of Fame, the Canadian Sports Hall of Fame, the Saskatchewan Hall of Fame, the Ontario Sport Legends Hall of Fame, the Providence Hall of Fame, the Cleveland Hall of Fame, the Prince Albert Hall of Fame and the Etobicoke Hall of Fame. That's one area where I think I've got the edge on my old buddy Gordie Howe.

When I look back on my career, I think more than anything, it was my work ethic that enabled me to persevere. I always strived toward hard work. I felt that what you do in practice, you'll do in the games. This is the way I was taught. I felt that to improve, you have to work hard. If you go through the motions, you're not going to get anywhere. Work at it and work at it and you'll improve yourself.

That's the way I was taught by my dad. He used to see me play in the backyard and at school. When I was late for supper, he'd come up to get me. When I left for Cleveland, he said, "You go there and you work hard and you'll be okay. But you've got to work hard." He was a laborer, he worked at hard labor his whole life. It was a good piece of advice from him.

Once I made the NHL for good with the Maple Leafs, there were a lot of guys I was fighting for a job. Every year, they tried to get my job away from me, but I wouldn't give it up. Gerry Cheevers, wasn't known for working hard in practice, but when he came to training camp, if I worked, he would work, because he wanted to stay in Toronto more than anything. I think that I inspired the other players a lot. They knew here I was, way up over their age. They're only 23 or 24 and they'd figure, "How can this old coot keep going as strong as he is?" It was just hard work and that's all. In the long run, my dad's advice, really paid off.

I was very lucky to come to Toronto and I can't say enough about the organization. Even today, every time I go to the Air Canada Centre, they treat me wonderfully and always make me feel welcome. When you're walking in there, the fans still recognize you, the pens come out and you can't say no. The people of Toronto have been so super to me over the years. It's such a great feeling. Deep in my heart I thank them all for that. I'm just so grateful.

When the Maple Leafs won the Stanley Cup in 1967, I grabbed two bottles of champagne. They were left in dressing room, so I took them and hid them behind my bench, then I took them home afterwards. Nancy marked on the label, "Do not open until the Leafs win the next Stanley Cup."

Nancy and I celebrated our 50th wedding anniversary on November 3, 1998 and we had a party at the house. I'm thinking, "What am I going to do to make this a special occasion?" and I thought, "You know what would be a nice touch? To open up one of those bottles of champagne for all those people who came down to the house." So we got it out and I got the wire off and I started pressing on the cork. Usually, when you open a bottle of champagne, it makes a big popping sound and then a nice stream of champagne comes out, but there was nothing in there. Three-quarters of the bottle was empty. It had evaporated. I said to Nancy, "You haven't been drinking this champagne, have you?" It was so funny, but it didn't taste too good. I've still got one more bottle left. That one's full, because I checked it and we're saving that one until the Leafs win the Stanley Cup.

I get asked all the time, "When are the Leafs going to win the Cup?" I always say "Be patient, give them time." And the response I've been getting lately is "Time? For crying out loud, it's been nearly 40 years."

All these years, still trying to win one, but I'm here to tell Maple Leafs fans that they shouldn't give up hope. If you maintain your beliefs, if you keep working toward your goal, anything is possible.

My story is living proof of that.

JOHNNY BOWER IS A GREAT BIG teddy bear. Since the first day that I met him, I've never heard anyone say a bad word about Johnny, which is sort of funny, because I'm usually the person who is the first to give him a ribbing. But after spending 11 years rooming together on road trips, I think I've earned that right to give it to him every so often.

Johnny is the nicest person I've ever met in the game of hockey and I was fortunate that we were able to spend so much time together over the years. He's a sweet guy and a terrific person and we are still, to this day, the best of friends. We're like brothers, although some people would say that the way we talk to each other we're more like a married couple. But it's by chance that we met at all.

Back in the fall of 1958, Johnny had to be convinced to join the Maple Leafs. He really wasn't interested in coming to Toronto. Instead, he thought he had a couple of seasons left in his career and wanted to play them all in Cleveland. What neither of us knew was that by accepting a contract with the Leafs, we would be living together for the better part of each of the next 11 winters.

We were roommates, great roommates, but the decision for us to room together on the road was not ours. It was a tradition for the captain of the Leafs and the starting goaltender to room together. This tradition dated back to long before I put on the blue and white jersey of the Maple Leafs for the first time. It was Conn Smythe's rule. He believed that the captain and the goaltenders were the two most important players on his team and that they should stay together on the road. Teeder Kennedy and Syl Apps both roomed with Turk Broda and when it was my turn to wear the captain's "C," my roommate was Johnny Bower.

So, in many ways, it was by good fortune that we got to spend the amount of time together that we did and that we became great buddies away from the rink. Don't let him know this, but I always felt that Johnny made up 50 per cent of our team, because no team can win the Stanley Cup without good goaltending. When he arrived at our training camp in 1958, he was a champion and brought along a winning attitude from his days in the AHL. He expected us to win every game every season and that helped the Maple Leafs turn the corner from being a decent team that hadn't won the Stanley Cup in nearly a decade, into a dynasty that ranks among the greatest teams in hockey history.

What is amazing about Johnny is that he was a better hockey player at the age of 40 than he was at 30. A lot of his success was due to his determination. He was by far the hardest-working member of our club and although he was the nicest, most easy-going player on the team, he was a workhorse. It is what drove him to be the best. He hated giving up a goal. He hated the thought of that puck sitting in HIS net. In the mid-1960s, when Terry Sawchuk joined our team, while the two of them worked very well together, they were polar opposites when it came to their work ethic. At the end of practice, we'd line up 100 pucks to shoot at each goaltender. We would have to go and get the 100 pucks out of Terry's net, but even if Johnny was beaten in practice, you wouldn't find a puck in his net. He'd clean out the goal as soon as the puck was behind him. He wouldn't let that little black piece of rubber spend one second more than necessary in his net.

One of the most vivid memories I have of Johnny comes from the 1962 Stanley Cup final. We were in Chicago for the fourth game of the series and Johnny was in his glory. He was so determined that he was going to help us win the Cup, that he was going to play at any cost. So it's the third period and he makes a sensational splits save. If you've ever seen video of how he played, he didn't just get up from the splits one leg at a time, he'd do this jackknife move that would allow him to get back into position quickly. The only problem was this time when he jackknifed himself up, he fell back down because he had pulled his hamstring.

I was sitting on the bench watching my teammate struggle to get back up and into position. He finally got back up and grabbed a hold of the post to stay in position, but when the puck was sent behind the net to the other corner and I saw him struggle to go from post-to-post, I turned to our coach Punch Imlach and said, "Bower's hurt." I watched him limp out to the top of the crease to make another sensational stop on a shot from the point. We both knew he was in bad shape.

When the whistle blew, Punch said to me, "Army, go and tell him I want to see him." Now Johnny, being the wily veteran that he was, he knew that if he came to the bench, he was going to be pulled.

So I skated over to the net and said, "Punch wants you to come to the bench." He replied, "I'm not going to the bench, I'm fine." We argued for a few moments, as I tried to convince him that he needed to go to talk to Imlach. This went on for a few moments before finally, I skated back to the bench and said to Punch, "He won't come out."

It wasn't very often that someone disobeyed a direct order from Imlach, let alone in the fourth game of the Stanley Cup Final. Punch told me to relay a message back to Bower that if he didn't come to the bench, he was going to be fined $500, which was a lot for a player back then.

Bower finally agreed to head over to the bench and Punch asked him, "How's your leg?" Johnny told him it was fine, but Punch told him that it wasn't and that Don Simmons was going in to replace him. It was the last time he was on the ice in that series, but Johnny had already put us on the road to capturing the Cup.

When I think about Johnny's greatest accomplishments, I remind myself that many of them have come away from the ice. He's raised a tremendous family with his darling wife Nancy. They have three great children and six grandchildren who are all wonderful people.

In many ways, that's why people who have never met him in person know he's a great person. He's radiates kindness. Those people who have only ever seen him on television, or heard him do an interview on the radio know instantly that he's one of the kindest, most gentle men around.

He's loyal to his friends, family and community. If someone needs help, Johnny is the first to volunteer. Sometimes, people forget that he's done so much for Toronto and the surrounding area in the community and that he's been involved in so many different charities, community fundraisers and organizations over the years. Sometimes, we just all take for granted someone like Johnny, who has a heart that always finds a way to give more than he can ever take back.

He is the greatest Maple Leaf of all time and it's because of everything that he stands for. Yes, he was a tremendous hockey player and team leader, but it's his caring, giving personality that has endeared him to millions of fans throughout Canada and the United States.

That's why we all love Johnny Bower. After all, who doesn't love a big teddy bear?

GEORGE ARMSTRONG
TORONTO MAPLE LEAFS CAPTAIN, 1958-1969

Johnny Bower Statistics

PROFESSIONAL HOCKEY TEAMS

MINOR LEAGUE:
Cleveland Barons, AHL (1945-46-1952-53; 1957-58)
Providence Reds, AHL (1945-46; 1955-56-1956-57)
Vancouver Canucks, WHL (1954-55)

NATIONAL HOCKEY LEAGUE:
New York Rangers (1953-54-1954-55; 1956-57)
Toronto Maple Leafs (1958-59-1969-70)

NHL STATISTICS:
Regular Season Games Played—552
Wins—250
Losses—195
Ties—90
Goals-Against Average—2.51
Shutouts—37

STANLEY CUP PLAYOFFS:
Games Played—74
Wins—35
Losses—34
Goals-Against Average—2.47
Shutouts—5

ACHIEVEMENTS AND HONORS

NHL:
Won four Stanley Cup titles with the Toronto Maple Leafs (1961-62, 1962-63, 1963-64, 1966-67)

Won the Vezina Trophy as the NHL's leading goaltender (1960-61)

Shared the Vezina Trophy as the NHL's leading goaltender with teammate Terry Sawchuk (1964-65)

Selected to NHL First All-Star Team (1960-61)

Played in four NHL All-Star Games (1961, 1962, 1963, 1964)

Holds the professional hockey record of 706 wins by a goaltender.

Led the NHL in games (70) and minutes (4200) played in 1953-54 with the New York Rangers.

Led the NHL in wins (33) in 1960-61 with the Leafs.

Led the NHL in goals-against average four times (1960-61, 1963-64, 1964-65, 1965-66), all with Toronto.

Led the Stanley Cup playoffs in shutouts three times (1962-63, 1963-64, 1966-67) and in GAA three times (1961-62, 1962-63, 1963-64), all with Toronto.

Won three J.P. Bickell Awards for outstanding contributions to the Toronto Maple Leafs (1960, 1964, and 1965).

Second all-time in Toronto Maple Leafs history in regular-season games (472), wins (220) and third all-time in shutouts (33) by a goalie.

Second all-time in Toronto Maple Leafs history in Stanley Cup games (74), wins (34) and shutouts (5) by a goalie.

Bower's recording of the children's Christmas song Honky The Christmas Goose, released in December, 1965, set a then-Canadian record by selling 40,000 albums.

Only Leaf goaltender to be selected to the NHL First All-Star Team in the past 50 years.

Bower and Sawchuk are the only Leafs goalies to win the Vezina Trophy in the past 51 years.

Bower's Maple Leafs No. 1 sweater hangs in a place of honor from the rafters of the Air Canada Centre.

Inducted into the Hockey Hall of Fame in 1976.

Bower is also enshrined in eight other sports halls—the Canada Sports Hall of Fame, the American Hockey League Hall of Fame, the Saskatchewan Hall of Fame, the Ontario Sport Legends Hall of Fame, the Providence Hall of Fame, the Cleveland Hall of Fame, the Prince Albert Hall of Fame and the Etobicoke Hall of Fame.

AMERICAN HOCKEY LEAGUE:

All-time AHL leader with 359 wins

All-time AHL leader with 45 shutouts

Established an AHL shutout sequence mark of 249:51 from November 27, 1957 to December 7, 1957

Two-time Calder Cup winner with the Cleveland Barons (1950-51, 1952-53)

Won the 1955-56 Calder Cup with the Province Reds

Only three-time winner of the Les Cunningham Award as MVP of the league (1955-56, 1956-57, 1957-58)

Three-time winner of the Harry (Hap) Holmes Memorial Award as the AHL's top goalie (1951-52, 1956-57, 1957-58)

Selected to the AHL First All-Star Team five times (1951-52, 1952-53, 1955-56, 1956-57, 1957-58)

Selected to the AHL Second All-Star Team in 1950-51

Led the AHL in wins four times (1949-50, 1950-51, 1952-53, 1955-56)

Led the AHL in shutouts three times (1949-50, 1952-53, 1957-58)

Led the AHL in GAA two times (1956-57, 1957-58)

Twice led the AHL in playoff wins (1952-53, 1955-56)

Twice led the AHL in playoff GAA (1952-53, 1955-56)

Led the AHL in playoff shutouts with four in 1952-53

Bower's No. 1 sweater was retired in 1997 by the Cleveland Barons

WESTERN HOCKEY LEAGUE:

Won the WHL leading goaltender award with the Vancouver Canucks in 1954-55

Led the WHL in shutouts (seven) and goals-against average (2.71) that same season

HIGHLIGHTS:

November 8, 1924—Johnny is born in Prince Albert, Saskatchewan.

1942—Johnny enlisted in the Canadian Armed Forces and was shipped overseas to England.

February 14, 1944—Johnny received an honorary discharge from the Canadian Armed Forces.

1944-45—Returned to play for the Prince Albert Hawks in the

Saskatchewan Junior League, when Johnny posted a league-leading 2.57 GAA. He also played for the Laura Beavers in the Memorial Cup playdowns.

1945—Johnny is signed to a pro contract by the Cleveland Barons, for a salary of $1700, including a $50 signing bonus.

October 16, 1945—Johnny made his AHL debut for Cleveland in a 4-3 loss to the Hershey Bears.

December 1, 1945—Johnny posted the first of an AHL-record 359 wins and a pro-hockey mark of 706 victories with a 4-3 verdict over the Providence Reds.

December 8, 1945—Blanked the Buffalo Bisons 2-0 for the first of a record 45 career AHL shutouts.

November 3, 1948—Johnny married the former Nancy Brain at noon at Cleveland's Trinity Church. Teammate Roy Kelly stood up as his best man.

1949-50—Johnny led the AHL in wins (38) and shutouts (5) with Cleveland.

1950-51—Johnny led the AHL with 44 wins for Cleveland. Backstopped the Barons to the Calder Cup championship. Named to the AHL Second All-Star Team.

1951-52—Johnny won Harry (Hap) Holmes Trophy as AHL's top goaltender with Cleveland. Named to the AHL's First All-Star Team.

1952-53—Johnny led the AHL with 40 wins and six shutouts. Named to the AHL's First All-Star Team. Backstopped Cleveland to another Calder Cup championship, defeating Pittsburgh 1-0 in a Game 7 overtime affair.

July 20, 1953—Johnny is traded by Cleveland (AHL) to the New York Rangers with Eldred Kobussen for Emile Francis, Neil Strain and cash.

October 8, 1953—Johnny made his NHL debut for the New York Rangers at Detroit's Olympia in 4-1 loss to the Red Wings

October 11, 1953—Johnny defeated Chicago 5-3 for his first NHL victory

January. 14, 1954—Johnny made 39 saves, 17 of them in the third period, to post his first NHL shutout, a 2-0 decision in Chicago.

January 30, 1954—Johnny was in goal for a 2-1 victory over the Montreal Canadiens, New York's first win at the Montreal Forum in 24 games.

March 11, 1954—Johnny and Nancy's son John is born in New York.

September 1954—Johnny is assigned by the New York Rangers to Vancouver of the WHL.

November 24, 1954—Johnny is recalled to the NHL by the New York Rangers for a five-game stint to fill in for injured goalie Gump Worsley.

1954-55—Johnny led the WHL in GAA (2.71) and posted a league record-tying seven shutouts for Vancouver.

September, 1956—Johnny is assigned by the New York Rangers to Providence (AHL).

1955-56—Johnny led the AHL with 45 regular-season wins and earned his first Les Cunningham Trophy as AHL MVP. Won Harry (Hap) Holmes Trophy as AHL's top goaltender. Named to the AHL's First All-Star Team. Finished as the playoff leader in wins (seven) and GAA (2.56) as Providence won the Calder Cup.

October 1956—Johnny backstopped Providence to a 4-0 shutout of the AHL All-Stars, the first shutout in AHL All-Star Game history.

March 10, 1957—Johnny blanked Rochester 8-0 for his AHL record-breaking 37th shutout.

1956-57—Johnny led the AHL with a 2.37 GAA and earned his second consecutive Les Cunningham Trophy as AHL MVP. Won Harry (Hap) Holmes Trophy as AHL's top goaltender. Named to the AHL's First All-Star Team. Named Providence's athlete of the year.

July 31, 1957—Johnny is traded by the New York Rangers to Cleveland (AHL) for Ed MacQueen.

November. 27, 1957—Johnny began his AHL record shutout sequence of 249:51 by keeping a clean sheet for the final 14:51 of a game versus Buffalo.

December 7, 1957—After three consecutive shutouts, Lou Jankowski scored on Johnny at 8:26 of the second period in Cleveland's 6-2 win over Buffalo. His shutout tally of 249.51 wiped out the mark of 221:02 established by Hershey's Nick Damore in 1939-40.

January 11, 1958—Johnny and Nancy's daughter Cindy is born in Cleveland.

1957-58—Johnny led the AHL with 8 shutouts and a 2.17 GAA and earned his third straight Les Cunningham Trophy as AHL MVP. Won Harry (Hap) Holmes Trophy as AHL's top goaltender. Named to the AHL's First All-Star Team.

June 3, 1958—Johnny is selected by Toronto Maple Leafs from Cleveland (AHL) in intra-league draft.

October 11, 1958—Johnny made his debut as a Leaf in a 3-1 loss to the Chicago Black Hawks at Maple Leaf Gardens.

October 18, 1958—Johnny defeated Boston Bruins 3-2 for his first victory as a Leaf.

March 24, 1959—Johnny made his Stanley Cup debut in a 5-1 loss at Boston.

March 28, 1959—Johnny posted his first Stanley Cup victory in a 3-2 overtime decision over the Bruins.

April 7, 1959—Johnny won his first Stanley Cup series, backstopping the Leafs to a 3-2 win at Boston in Game 7 of their semifinal series.

April 9, 1959—Johnny made his Stanley Cup final debut, losing a 5-3 decision to the Canadiens at Montreal.

April 14, 1959—Johnny recorded a 3-2 overtime victory over Montreal for his first Stanley Cup final victory.

April 7, 1960—Johnny backstops the Leafs to their second straight Stanley Cup final appearance, but Toronto is swept in four games by Montreal.

May 23, 1960—Johnny and Nancy's daughter Barbara is born in Toronto.

March 19, 1961—Johnny is awarded the Vezina Trophy after recording the NHL's lowest goals-against average. Also selected to the NHL's First All-Star Team.

October 7, 1961—Johnny played for the NHL All-Stars as they defeated the Stanley Cup champion Black Hawks 3-1 in the All-Star Game at Chicago Stadium.

April 15, 1962—Johnny posted his first Stanley Cup shutout, earning a 3-0 victory over the Black Hawks at Chicago Stadium in Game 2 of the Cup final series.

April 22, 1962—Johnny won his first Stanley Cup as the Leafs downed Chicago 2-1 in Game 6 of the final series.

October 6, 1962—Johnny backstopped the Leafs to a 4-1 decision over the All-Stars in the NHL All-Star Game at Maple Leaf Gardens.

March 20, 1963—Johnny earned a 3-3 tie against Montreal to help Toronto clinch first place in the NHL standings for the first time since the 1947-48 season.

April 18, 1963—Johnny posted a 3-1 victory over Detroit in Game 5 of the final series against the Detroit Red Wings to give Toronto its second straight Stanley Cup.

October 5, 1963—Johnny held the All-Stars to a 3-3 tie in the NHL All-Star Game at Maple Leaf Gardens.

April 7, 1964—With Toronto facing elimination in Game 6 of their semifinal series against Montreal, Johnny stops 25 shots in a 3-0 shutout win over the Habs.

April 9, 1964—Blocking 38 of 39 shots, Johnny carries Toronto to a 3-1 decision over Montreal in Game 7 of their semifinal series, earning the Leafs their third successive trip to the Stanley Cup finals and fifth in six seasons.

April 25, 1964—Johnny posted a 4-0 shutout over Detroit in Game 7 of the final series to give the Leafs their third Stanley Cup in as many seasons.

October 10, 1964—Johnny dropped a 3-2 decision to the All-Stars in the annual NHL All-Star Game at Maple Leaf Gardens.

November 8, 1964—The oldest active NHL player, Johnny celebrated his 40th birthday.

March 28, 1965—Johnny stops all 37 shots he faces in a 4-0 win at Detroit to clinch the Vezina Trophy for him and teammate Terry Sawchuk.

December 27, 1965—Johnny's rendition of the children's Christmas song Honky The Christmas Goose reaches No. 29 on the CHUM charts in Toronto.

It sells 40,000 albums, which at the time made Honky the biggest-selling Canadian-made record.

April 3, 1966—Playing the first period of a 3-3 tie at Detroit, Johnny is part of NHL history as the Leafs become the first team to use three goalies in a game. Terry Sawchuk (second period) and Bruce Gamble (third period) also played.

April 22, 1967—Johnny made 31 saves as Toronto blanked Montreal 3-0 in Game 2 of the Stanley Cup final.

April 24, 1967—Johnny blocked 54 shots in a 3-2 double-overtime decision over the Canadiens in Game 3 of the final.

May 2, 1967—A 3-1 victory over the Canadiens in Game 6 of the final series gives Johnny his fourth Stanley Cup title.

1968-69—After 23 pro seasons of playing without a mask, Johnny finally dons facial protection for the final 17 games of the season.

April 6, 1969—Johnny gets the starting nod in a 3-2 loss to Boston in what will be his final Stanley Cup game. At 44 years, four months and 28 days of age, he's the oldest goalie ever to appear in a Stanley Cup game.

November 8, 1969—Johnny celebrates his 45th birthday and becomes the first NHLer to be eligible to collect his league pension while still an active player.

December 10, 1969—Johnny makes his farewell NHL appearance in a 6-3 loss at Montreal at the age of 45 years, one month and two days.

March 19, 1970—Johnny announced his retirement as an active player to accept a position as a scout and goaltender coach with the Leafs.

August 26, 1976—Johnny is inducted into the Hockey Hall of Fame.

January 9, 1980—The Leafs sign Johnny, 55, to an NHL contract for one dollar to serve as a standby goaltender after Leafs goalies Mike Palmateer and Paul Harrison are unable to play. Rookie Vincent Tremblay arrives from Moncton of the AHL in time to play the game and although he's dressed and ready to go in the Leafs dressing room, Johnny doesn't see any action.

1988—Inducted into the Saskatchewan Hall of Fame.

July 18, 1990—After 32 years with the Toronto Maple Leafs as a goaltender, assistant coach and scout, Johnny announces his retirement from the organization.

1995—The Toronto Maple Leafs recognize Johnny and fellow Leafs Hall of Fame goalie Walter (Turk) Broda by hanging the No. 1 sweater each wore in a place of honor from the rafters at Maple Leaf Gardens.

1999—Johnny is inducted into the Canada Sports Hall of Fame.

2000—Johnny is presented the Mel Osborne Fellowship by the Kiwanis Club of Credit Valley, Ontario, an award which honors people for their contribution to the community. He is just the second person outside the Kiwanis Club to receive the award. The first was actor Roger Moore.

November, 2001—Johnny's No. 1 sweater is retired by the AHL's Cleveland Barons.

2003—Johnny is named an honorary police chief by the Peel, Ontario Regional Police Force.

January 5, 2006—Johnny is among seven hockey legends named as part of inaugural induction class into the American Hockey League Hall of Fame.

A MESSAGE FROM THE PUBLISHER

We are very proud to present the extraordinary story of the legendary Johnny Bower in *The China Wall*. Bob Duff has artfully crafted the remarkable life of one of Hocky's all time favorite sport's heroes. We are supremely grateful to Johnny and his lovely wife, Nancy. Also, we appreciate the Bower family and their other special friends for their unique input and participation. Immortal Investments is honored to present *The China Wall*. It will inspire readers now and in future generations. God Bless!

Michael J. Reddy
Publisher

Immortal Investments Publishing produces timeless books that move, inspire, and spotlight the best of the human spirit manifested by extraordinary human achievement.

Please review and order our other outstanding titles by visiting www.immortalinvestments.com or by calling **1-800-475-2066.**

Please let us know if you have suggestions for other exceptional books or have comments about ***The China Wall.***

***This publishing venture is revolutionary in that the book like all other Immortal Investment titles is not distributed to bookstores. It is available exclusively through Immortal Investments Publishing.

To bring Johnny Bower to your event for a personal book signing please contact www.immortalinvestments.com.

Order your signed copy by
Johnny Bower today!
1-800-475-2066.
NOT SOLD IN BOOKSTORES

Immortal Investmants Publishing
35122 W. Michigan Ave. Wayne, MI 48184

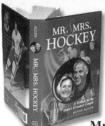
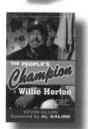

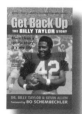

boji books PRESENTS...

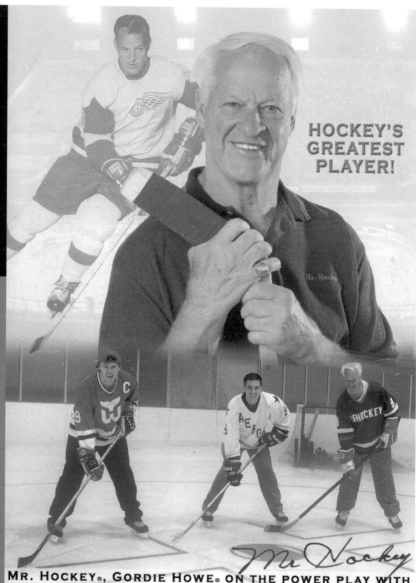

STRESSED OUT FROM DEADLINES?
WE TAKE THE PRESSURE OFF YOU!

- 1-4 Color Printing
- Creative Design
- Perfect Impressions

Creative Impressions
Printing & Graphics
(248) 435-0800

"For A Perfect Impression,
See for Yourself..."